What You Must Know
When You Travel With a
CAMERA

by

SAMUEL E. LESSERE

(Fifth revised and enlarged edition)

Copyright 1963: Harian Publications, Greenlawn, New York

Trade Distributor: Crown Publishers, Inc.

TABLE OF CONTENTS

Your Trip Abroad Can Last Indefinitely   3

What to Shoot Abroad   5
- You Can Find Out Where the Pictures Are   5
- Helpful Photo Clubs Abroad   5
- Photo Magazines Abroad Which Will Supply Up-to-the-Minute Photo Tips   6
- Children Are Trumps   6
- Your Own Profession or Business Can Yield the Finest Pictures   7

You'll Take Better Pictures If You Remember the Following   15
- Your Pictures Can Tell the Story of Your Travels   15
- "Posed" Versus Natural Travel Shots   15
- When Candid Tricks May Be Needed   15
- "Framing" Your Shot   17

Easy Picture-Taking Guide for Beginners   18

Quick Hints for Better Pictures   20
- Know Your Equipment   27

Would You Like to Make Your Pictures Outstanding Pictures?   29
- Well—Here Are a Few Hints   29
- Museum Interiors   32
- Bridges Are Pictorial   33
- Take Pictures of the Choo-Choo Trains   34
- Monuments—Walled Towns   35
- Picturesque Canals   37
- Tricky Interior Exposures   38

Action Photography — from Airplane, Train, Bus, Auto, Ship, etc.   40
- Pictures From an Airplane   42
- Filtering in Aerial Photography   43
- The Camera Must Be Steady   43
- Shooting from Airliners   43
- Shutter Speeds and Focusing   45
- Aerial Movies   45
- Pictures Taken on or From a Moving Ship   46
- Photographing From a Bus   46
- Pictures From a Train   47
- Pictures From an Auto   48
- Technical Data for Guidance in Taking Action Shots   49

The Sequential Picture Story   51
- What Does the Story-Telling Technique Demand   51

Flash Photography is a Cinch   54
- How to Determine Your Flash Exposures   59
- Film & Flashbulb Guide   60

What to Do About Climatic Conditions (Some Precautions)   62
- Film Precautions   63
- Climate Also Affects Picture-taking   64

Beware of Photographing Those "Illegal" Shots   65

Processing Your Film When You Travel   68
- Some Additional Processing Hints   70
- Causes and Prevention of Print Defects   70
- If You Can Do Your Own Processing   71
- Common Faults in Negatives   72
- Photo Dealers and Processing Establishments   73
- Color Processing Outside U.S.   75

What Equipment Should You Take?   76
- The Camera   76
- The Box Camera   77
- The Miniature Camera   77
- Interchangeable Lenses   79
- The Square Format Camera   81
- Special Backs   82
- Candid Techniques with the Reflex Camera   83
- The Folding Camera   83
- The Larger Cameras   83
- Polaroid-Land Camera   84

Film and Accessories   85
- Film Comes in Numerous Varieties   86
- Guide to Choosing Black and White Film   87
- Filter and Other Accessories   88
- Exposure Meter Techniques   90
- Carry-All Case   92
- Should You Use a Tripod?   92
- Lens Tissue   94
- Is Your Equipment in Perfect Condition?   94

Camera "Buys" in Foreign Countries   95

Are You Traveling with a Movie Camera?   99

Movie-Making Equipment to Take with You   103
- Magazine Loading   103
- Movie-Making Accessories   104

Going Through Customs — At Home and Abroad   106
- Customs Regulations of Various Foreign Countries with Respect to Photographic Equipment   108

How to Insure Your Photographic Equipment Against Loss or Damage   112

Section of General Technical Data   115
- Table of Lens Openings and Exposure Factors   117
- Basic Daylight Exposure for most commonly used films   118
- Guide to f/ Numbers to be used in conjunction with Flash Guide Numbers   119
- Exposure Table for Photoflood Lamps   120
- Most Popular Film Speeds   121
- Instructions for Processing Color Film   123
- Toning Prints   125

YOUR TRIP ABROAD CAN LAST

INDEFINITELY

One thing is certain: You will never get as much satisfaction from any pictures you ever made before as you will from those you'll take abroad.

What will most interest and excite you about your trip abroad will be the exotic picturesque color all about you. The color of the landscape will, somehow, be different from that which you are accustomed to at home. Nor will color be the only feature to entrance you. The natives, in their local costumes, will excite your pictorial attention. Even their every-day clothes will be enough different to be of superb interest, while their holiday clothes will retain all the traditional flavor of the ages. Some don't even know modernism exists.

In addition to all that, there will be the novel architecture of the buildings and cathedrals, ranging from Romanesque through Gothic and Baroque; the scenic wonders, both natural and man-made; pyramids, quaint bridges, fortresses, castles, the cute little passenger trains with their car-long outside sightseeing corridors, and their swift, modern brothers, the "rapides"; the busy and fascinating markets; the ancient battlefields and ruins; all these vivid and mysterious things demand a camera so they may be recorded for your personal pleasure forever.

Some of these scenes will demand the use of color, some a quick black and white snapshot; some will have action which compellingly suggests motion pictures. Each of these effects is a technique of its own and each is most appropriate to its own field.

I do not suggest that you equip yourself with apparatus appropriate to all these techniques, though there are those to whom neither time nor money is an object who will do just that. Indeed, I've seen tourists so loaded down with equipment that the natives' eyes goggled at the sight. Mine too — it must be added. However, recommendations about cameras and techniques will be given in some detail elsewhere to enable the beginner to make his own choice for the trip, if he has not already done so.

4   *What You Must Know When You Travel With A Camera*

Photo by Hamilton Wright

WHAT TO SHOOT ABROAD

Of the principal "sights" it must be said that, unless you have a special way of photographing them or wish to tie them up with members of your party (the usual thing), you would be better off buying the picture postcards that you will find for sale at the spot. In fact, you'll buy some postcards anyway.

Usually, these commercial postcards are not only better pictures than you can take — the professional photographers who do them are the crack photographers of the region and have all the time and facilities available for their purpose — but they are cheaper as well, when everything is considered.

Notwithstanding this, there are tremendous picture possibilities for the tourist in foreign countries, apart from the so-called "sights" located there. Each region has its own attractive specialties and it becomes an important part of your trip to find them.

You Can Find Out Where the Pictures Are

It is not necessary to squander your time (which, presumably, is not plentiful) aimlessly looking for these subjects. Regional camera clubs can easily be found whose members know all the best spots, many of them completely neglected by tourists, and these local amateurs will be eager to tell you about them.

HELPFUL PHOTO CLUBS ABROAD

AUSTRIA
Verband der Amatuerphotographer-Vereine Oesterreiches, Piaristengasse 11-20, Vienna.
BELGIUM
Fotoclub Vooruit, Niewland 37, Ghent
CUBA
Photo-Amateur Club, O'Reilly 366, Havana
DENMARK
Kobenhavns Fotografiske Amatorklub, H.C. Orstedsvej 22A, Copenhagen
GERMANY
Verband Deutscher Amateur-Fotografen Vereine, Kleverstrasse 76, Dusseldorf
Photo-Amateur Club, Herzog-Julius-Strasse 70, Bad Harzburg
Bregenzer Photo Club, Heldengang-Strasse 56, Bregenz-Vorkloster
ITALY
Cine Club ICAL di Milano, Milan
Cine Club, Salerno, Salerno
Associazione Fotografica Romana, Rome
Club Spilimbergo
Circolo Fotografica Reggino, Reggio-Calabria

JAPAN
Pleasant Club, 4, Ryogoku, Nihombashi, Tokyo
Nippon Shashin-kai, 3 7-chome Nishi-Ginza, Tokyo
Tampai Photo Club, 2, 3-chome, Kitahoriedori, Osaka
NETHERLANDS
Zeister Fotoclcub, (Zeist)
Utrecht A.F.V., Utrecht
A.F.V., Marnixstraat 406, Amsterdam
Haagse Fotoring, Hague
NORWAY
National Asso. Norwegian Amateur Photographers, Ovre Slottsgate 8, Oslo
GREECE
Elliniki Fotographiki Etaireia Asso., 39 Panepistimiou Ave., Athens
SWEDEN
Fotografiska Foreningen, Tunnelgatan 17, Stockholm
SWITZERLAND
Swiss Photo Club, DuPont Restaurant, Beatenplatz, Zurich
Schweizerische Fotografen-Bund, Zurich 23

Where a photo club does not exist there will nearly always be found a local photographer or camera shop. Invariably I have found them to be eager to cooperate and their familiarity with the local scene and conditions is invaluable. Consult them without hesitation. Frequently, I've encountered local photographers who closed up shop and insisted on going along on photo trips, with no thought of "poirboire" or "Trinkgeld." The open sesame is friendliness and a cheerful smile — these qualities grease a lot of doors abroad.

Other excellent sources of information about picture possibilities are the native photo magazines for amateurs. Every country has at least one such publication; some European countries (especially Great Britain) have several.

PHOTO MAGAZINES ABROAD WHICH WILL SUPPLY UP-TO-THE-MINUTE PHOTO TIPS

AUSTRIA
Oesterreichische Foto Zeitung, Richtergasse 4, Vienna
Foto-Digest, Linke Wienzeile 36, Vienna

BELGIUM
Photorama, Mortsel-Anvers
Photo-Monde, 13 rue les Sables, Brussels
Photo-Service, 27 rue Spte, Mortsel-les-Anvers

CZECHOSLOVAKIA
Ceskoslvenska Fotografie, Prague

DENMARK
Dansk Fotografisk Tidsskrift, Mynstersvej 14, Copenhagen
Focus, Tornebuskegade 1, Copenhagen

FRANCE
Photo Cine Revue, 118 rue d'assas, Paris
Photographe, 187 rue Sainte-Jacques, Paris
Science et Industrie Photographique, Paris

GREAT BRITAIN
Amateur Photographer, Dorset House, Stamford St., London
Camera World, Fountain Press
Good Photography, 123 Queen Victoria St., London
Miniature Camera Magazine, 9 Cavendish Sq., London
Miniature Camera World, 24 Store St., London
Photography, 20 Tudor St., London
British Journal of Photography, 24 Wellington St., London

GERMANY
Photo Magazin, International Edition, Munich 22, Bavaria
Photo-Post, Heidelberg 17a
Leica Fotographie, Frankfurt
Photofreund, Berlin
Grossbildtechnik, Munich

ITALY
Progresso Fotografice, Viale Romagna 53, Milan
Ferrania, Corso Matteotti 12, Milan
Fotografia, Milan
Revista Fotografica Italiana, Milan

NETHERLANDS
Foto, Telgen 8, Hengelo

SWEDEN
Foto, Luntmakaregatan 25, Stockholm

SWITZERLAND
Der Photo-Amateur, Zurichstr. 3, Lucerne
Camera, Zurichstr. 3, Lucerne

If you have the time, write the editor of such a magazine for information. If the publication happens to be located in the city you are visiting at the moment, drop in to see him — you might be agreeably surprised by what your inquiry might produce.

Among the subjects that are much more interesting than sights are numerous religious and patriotic festivals. While most of these occur in the spring, they are likely to occur at any time of the year. These offer colorful and exotic scenes that cannot be equalled at any other time or occasion.

Children Are Trumps

If you attend any of the festivals here mentioned or not, there is one subject that holds the greatest interest for everyone. That subject is children. Invariably, children are a part of the various civic and religious spectacles throughout the world. It is fortunate that this is so because they constitute the most enchanting part of these spectacles.

Normally, children are easier to photograph with the "candid" technique than adults. If they become accustomed to your presence, they will exhibit no self-consciousness at all, and you can almost poke the camera in their faces.

And shoot lots of film. The more shots you take the greater become your chances that you'll score. Professionals do that all the time.

What to Shoot Abroad

After the shower — Madeira Photo Samuel E. Lessere

**Your Own Profession or Business
Can Yield the Finest Pictures**

(Make Use of Your Special Advantages)

If you have a field of special interest, whether it be that of work or play, the pictures you take reflecting that interest will most certainly be of future value to you, from any standpoint. If your knowledge of the particular specialty is applied to the taking of pictures, you will enjoy a tremendous advantage over other photographers who do not share that knowledge.

8 *What You Must Know When You Travel With A Camera*

The principle is that the *field you know best will yield the pictures you take best.*

An architect, for example may take pictures of special architectural value, either for his own collection or for sale to architectural trade journals. Since Europe and the Mediterranean region are the very cradle of the architecture of our Western world, the possibilities here are endless. A camera with a rising and falling front, and adjustable back, will be needed to secure accurate perspective for this kind of work. It is no field for the beginner, generally speaking.

A botanist, also, would suffer from an *embarras de richesse.* The island of Madeira alone would furnish him with activity it would take more than a year to exploit to a full degree. Here the best type of camera would be a plate camera with ground glass back for fine focusing; and double extension bellows, for close work and copying. Such pictures are of greatest value when the tiniest detail is clearly recorded.

Archeology, of course, is a world apart. A specialist in this field will never be caught with his lens down, so to speak, and he is likely to boast really professional equipment and know-how.

A student or teacher of history would also have a field day. He need only consult regional guidebooks to be steered to scenes of historical interest unparalled in our young country. In our own recent past we have become so intimately associated with the battlefields of Europe that their history now impinges on ours, and is, in fact, a part of our own historical tradition.
In some of these well-known and often visited places, the tourist might well save a good part of his film. More than likely, there will be found on sale at these historic sites, picture postcards frequently better and, in any case, cheaper than the tourist can shoot for himself. Of course if he plans to sell pictures, they must be his own.

A physician could take many pictures of hospitals abroad. Not that these hospitals are better or have superior techniques to ours—usually the contrary is true. The pictures can, however, be of interest in showing the contrast with our institutions. One exception, to my own knowledge, comes to mind. The Hospital Maternidad, in Mexico City, operated by the Mexican Social Security Administration, is in advance of any hospital I've seen anywhere in the world. It is one of Mexico's prime exhibits yet tourists rarely see it or, if they do, it is from the outside only. Yet you are free to enter and take all the pictures you want. Flash or floodlights necessary.

An advertising man abroad would have himself a picnic. If there is anything left in the world that has not yet evolved into dull un-

A view of the Lofoten Island, the home of the largest cod fisheries, North Norway.

iformity, it is poster design. An expert can even recognize the origin of any particular poster, so accurately do these ubiquitous forms of advertising reflect the character of their nativity. Since most of these posters are displayed outdoors, in good light, there is no trick at all to their successful photography. Incidentally, the cost of the film and the processing should be an acceptable deductible item on the income tax report, as a business expense.

For a physical director, what would be more interesting than a series of pictures of youth sports and calisthenics abroad. Every country has its share of this form of activity. While the nature of the activities in this field does not differ from ours to any material extent, the picture of a group of Japanese or Malayan or Italian or Swedish children going through setting-up exercises can have a very special charm. And how easy to sell to a journal of education or, with an accompanying article, to publications in related fields.

Interior Decorators. Since our country borrows its decorative motifs from every country in the world, it is professionally profitable to study the various decorative schemes in the countries in which they originated. The photographs will constitute permanent records and may be a valuable business asset.

Antique dealers. Same as above.

Costume designers. European style still leads and the roving American designer finds his camera very useful. More enterprising ones find that the Orient can inspire some striking new ideas. And adaptations from Central American native costumes are also infiltrating the U. S.

Fashion designers. As above.

Theatre people. Of great interest for show people would be the performances and ancient folk dances often given among the ruins of Rome and the Grecian ruins in Sicily and Athens. Carnival and circus people might use their cameras freely at the open-air acts given in Parisian streets and by small traveling groups in Spain and Morocco. Permission might also be obtained for taking pictures inside theatres in France and England, though usually not permitted.

Directors of parks and zoos. Open-air zoos, without cages or apparent separation from visitors, originated in Africa (the National Parks) and Europe. In addition, Europe has some of the loveliest cultivated parks in the world. Gardens in Madeira and the Canary Islands, while not so sophisticated, have natural beauties of their own. Lisbon houses a beautiful horticultural palace, as does Monte Carlo; and the Kew Gardens in London are known throughout the world. All these are fabulous targets for the photographer whose interest they are.

Pharmacists. Will be fascinated by the variety and the quaintness of appearance of the *farmacia, drogueria, Apotheke, vaistine,* abroad.

Farmers. Soil is soil is soil. But farmers will marvel at the varying and sometimes crude techniques used by farmers in foreign lands. It may astonish our farmers to learn that, given the conditions, some of these crude techniques cannot be improved upon. But they are interesting to photograph and good pictures in this field have a wide American market among our numerous farm papers which go in for pictorial treatment.

Religious people. Not only will they find interest in visiting the origin of their own beliefs, but the beliefs of others. In many countries, churches, temples, and monasteries are more numerous than bathrooms. Religious leaders boast costumes, too, of great variety and magnificence.

Educators. The most cordial, the most hospitable people in the world are educators. An interest in pedagogy will get you a cordial welcome everywhere and special pains will be taken to show you everything. Even if you are not specially interested in education, try that approach and see the doors fly open. *You'll get interested.* Photographing the children in their classes and in their playgrounds will keep you busy. Handicraft schools are extremely interesting. Take pictures of the native children at work in these craft activities.

Anthropologists. These specialists will have wonderful opportunities to picture the customs and costumes of a wide variety of native peoples. Despite the world's modernity, a surprising number of peoples of the world still adhere to ancient traditions. Pictures of these exert a great charm for Americans.

Business men. An American business man will get almost the same kind of welcome as an educator. There will be a touch of envy in his reception but it will be tacit. Pictures of business contacts you'll make abroad will be a long-appreciated memory, might even yield a profit.

Art directors, curators, art students and art lovers. To disclose that you're in the art profession, if you wish to photograph the inside of museums, may actually prove a disadvantage unless you have influential friends and assured contacts. Best go incognito. You will then have the same chance to photograph that is open to laymen. In most European museums, photography is not permitted. But, throughout France, at any rate, permission can be obtained. This is especially true of the famous Louvre in Paris. A small extra fee is exacted for the privilege of using a hand-held camera. For the use of a tripod and/or flash, special permission must be obtained. The lighting and hanging of the paintings have been greatly improved so that the available light and the use of a tripod will be sufficient for most amateur purposes. The same conditions obtain for museum interiors and chateaux interiors throughout France. In some cases, permission to use a tripod can be obtained only for non-visiting hours.

Librarians. In most instances, same provisions as for art curators.

Printers. That's *my* alley. The important type foundries are to be found only in Europe, specifically France, Germany, and Holland. There are foundries too, of lesser importance, in England, Spain, Austria and Italy. Printers are welcome in all of them. Welcome too, in some ancient European printshops which still exist and where crude but charming handwork still prevails. The oldest printshop in Spain is still operating in Mallorca, and under the ownership of descendants of the original owners. Gutenburg's followers are friendly to a degree and once you've made a contact with any of them, you'll find it very difficult to break away.

Railroad men. If you're a VIP, you can gain wonderful contacts. If just a working stiff, you will still find the cute foreign trains wonderful objects for your camera. If you're a model train fan (the most fanatic fans in the world — I have one in my family), you will investigate the model trains made in Germany, the finest in the world. The enthusiasts in England are organized in very intensive fashion. In Paris, contact the Assoc. Francaise des Amis des Chemins de Fer, 2 Rue de Poissy. Ask to see their marvelous operating layout at 48 Blvd. de Clichy. You will be allowed to operate it too. There will be a small fee.

Spelaelogist (cave man). That's right. If you're interested in caves —and there are such lunatics in all countries—(it's a special taste). you can make the necessary contact through regional tourist offices. There exist special facilities for underground photography and you will be given cordial assistance by the small groups that go in for this fantastic activity. It's not feasible to feign an interest in this activity for the adventure, because it involves a specialized jargon which cannot easily be faked.

Ships and boats. The varieties of boats, working and sport, are amazing in number. If you are interested, just go to any harbor and everything to delight your heart lies right in front of you. If the harbor is any kind of a naval port, better get official advice beforehand. Many boat-owners will be flattered by your interest, will want to buy your shots. An opportunity for Polaroid owners.

Sea diving. This is a new craze that has enveloped Europe. It follows the development of apparatus that enables anyone to pierce sea depths to an extent that, hitherto, had been possible only for professional divers, using elaborate equipment. Now, the amateur diver needs no assistant but can go down by himself and stay down for an hour or more. You can picture such a diver in his descent and ascent and photograph, too, the objects that he may bring up from the depths. The Riviera is the likeliest region for this sort of photography.

Castles. If that's your interest you have plenty of work ahead. And you'd better have stout legs. Picturesque castles are rarely found in the middle of towns, so fairly elaborate excursions are usually necessary. In the Orient and Central America, where ancient temples lie hidden in inaccessible regions, you will require guides and detailed preparations. The castles of Europe contain historical furniture styles and one in Lisbon holds the largest collection of decorative old horse-drawn carriages in the world.

WHAT TO SHOOT ABROAD

Photo Samuel E. Lessere
A fishing boat off Tangiers, Morocco. Guess what the eye is for?

Tapestry and rug weaving. It is said that this field is a very fascinating one. The examples I've seen left me unimpressed. But then I'm not an expert. You will be allowed to visit the famous European tapestry factories—don't overlook the Gobelin factory in France. I doubt that you'll be allowed to take photographs—European industrialists are more secretive than Americans. In the Orient and Morocco, where much of the weaving is done outdoors, photography may be easier but I suspect it had better be done inconspicuously.

Wood carving. A wonderful handicraft pursued with fervor in the Swiss & Austrian Tyrol.

There are hundreds of activities and hobbies other than the ones I've mentioned. Most foreign countries are less intensively industrialized than we are and they retain handicraft techniques to a greater extent than we do. As a result you will come across the pursuit of hobbies and handicrafts in what would seem to us an amazing variety, some of them quite unknown to us.

Pictures of unusual hobbies and handicraft skills have a wide and ready market in U.S. and it should be comparatively easy for an industrious photographer to get a full bag of them. It's a subject that lends itself to the technique of series pictures, so popular with picture news magazines. That is, you can start with a picture of the raw material and the craftsman setting it up for work; then take a picture of each successive stage in the process. You wouldn't have the slightest difficulty selling such a series.

To get the pictures you want in any of the various fields mentioned, the important, the indispensable quality demanded is tact and friendliness. Most people do not mind being photographed, especially if they are convinced that the picture is not being taken for some idle purpose or to satisfy a tourist's whim, but out of a real knowledge or enthusiastic interest in their activities.

American prestige in the world today is such that foreigners are flattered by the attention you give them or the thought that they are of some value to you. It is well not to overdo this advantage, but it does exist and a very useful one it is.

Official tourist bureaus will cooperate enthusiastically—that's what they're in business for—and they will go to any trouble to help you. Tourists usually do not make enough use of them. They are most likely to know where you can get the pictures you want and can furnish the special contacts you may need. An American is *persona grata* to a high degree, and often is given the use of facilities not even available to natives of the country.

A final point:—Do not fail to make notes of all the pictures you take, including such relevant details as the place, the date, and all other particulars in connection with each photo. It may not seem important to do this at the moment and it may seem a nuisance to use up your precious travel time for the purpose, but the information may become valuable later, after you have returned from the trip.

You may decide, when back home, to make up an album in sequence, for which purpose the notes you record will be indispensable. The notes, combined with the photos, would then constitute a running diary of the trip. In addition, should any of the photos be acceptable for a commercial purpose, the pertinent information will be an essential requirement—you cannot rely on your memory for that purpose.

YOU'LL TAKE BETTER PICTURES IF YOU REMEMBER THE FOLLOWING

Your Pictures Can Tell the Story of Your Travels

It seems fulsome to emphasize that you must try to make your pictures say something, that they should have some meaning for others than your own immediate family circle or friends. One of the most frequently reproduced pictures — one that everyone must have seen at some time or other — is a very simple picture indeed. It shows a little girl selling flowers in the street. With one hand the child extends the flowers while with the other she makes an appealing sales gesture that conveys a universal story of charm. Obviously, it is not a posed shot nor could it have been difficult to take. Foreign scenes abound in such possibilities that are not beyond the capabilities of the average photographer. Such a picture pays off every time.

Posed Shots Should Be Avoided

Posed shots, faces almost poked into the camera, are not of great value, unless you are a professional with long experience in posing models and are able to get them to register spontaneity of expression.

When Candid Tricks May Be Needed

It is best to shoot candid. That is, try to get your shot while the subject is unaware of what you are doing and doesn't "freeze up," to use an expression coined by photographers when people stiffen up and assume unnatural poses while their pictures are being taken.

Of course, if you are uncertain about candid results, you can get people to pose for you; generally those who are willing to pose expect a gratuity. While you might not begrudge the gratuity, it does take the charm out of the situation. Besides, the fact that pictures posed for by the ordinary people you might encounter in this informal manner are rarely of much pictorial value.

While it is possible for the amateur to get picturesque views of natives by shooting those he encounters informally, it is a painful duty in disillusionment to report that the exotic natives frequently shown in magazines are professional models who have trained for a good part of their lives to look unposed.

With a little practice, candid photography is no more difficult than any other kind, especially with the use of a fast lens, and it is a good deal more exciting. You focus in advance and make all the other necessary settings on the camera: shutter speed and lens opening. Then, in a relaxed attitude, you point the lens at the object, very casually, and face and look off in another direction altogether. You will find that most people will not take notice that the *lens* is pointed at *them* instead of the direction in which you are looking.

Children, once they are used to your presence, will not notice you at all. If children do notice you, they, like the adults mentioned above, will be inclined to look in the direction you are looking, paying no attention to the camera lens pointed at them—it's your *direction* they'll be looking at. It's an old trick and still works like a charm. Incidentally, a reflex camera is a "natural" for this technique. There are several small cameras which have, as accessory, oblique view finders that almost take a picture around a corner. Voigtlander is one of them.

Scenic vistas are most effective if a human being or an animal is in the picture somewhere. Nothing is so bald as a landscape with no living thing in sight. Besides, something is needed to give scale. If you do include a living creature in the scene, you must determine what the important feature of the shot is to be: the scene or the figure, and "frame" (compose) the picture accordingly. It's not as difficult as it sounds; it merely means that you shift your camera position to meet the pictorial requirements.

With some action shots, it's best not to "stop" the action. A running stream looks a lot more natural if some movement is apparent; if the action, in short, is not "frozen."

About composition there are so many conflicting opinions—every teacher of photography has his own individual ideas about the subject—that composition has become a bugaboo for beginners.

My own opinion, for whatever it is worth, is that amateurs should not bedevil themselves about composition when *taking* the picture. There are enough factors to contend with in the process of taking a picture without fussing about that added complication.

My counsel, regardless of what others may say, is that you just go ahead and take whatever pictures appeal to you and from whatever angle that looks good at the moment.

Later, when the film has been developed and a contact print of a certain shot still looks good to you, you can "crop" to eliminate distracting elements when having the enlargement made.

If you follow this practice, you have a better chance to form an interesting composition than you would during the excitement of the actual picture-taking. Not only do you then have a better chance to study your subject but more time and steadier nerves as well.

The difficulty with trying for an artistic composition while taking the picture is that not all scenes will stand still while you study the composition — the world does move. I recall a fussy amateur friend, never without a tripod and scads of equipment, who once took 30 minutes to set up his apparatus and to frame his composition for a shot of a sunset. Unfortunately, unlike Joshua, he could not command the sun to stand still. When he was ready to snap, there was nothing to snap—there was no sunset; it was nightfall.

It does not pay to be as fussy as all that because there is really no difficulty in taking interesting travel pictures without the fuss. Indeed, if there's any difficulty, it's in the matter of selection from the bewildering possible choices of scene and subject. In most cases, the scenes are so spectacular the picture almost selects itself.

"Framing" Your Shot

A little pictorial trick that will serve to enhance the value of your pictures is to give them their own natural "frame." This is a simple trick—one that is commonly employed by crack professional photographers—and, once it has been brought to your attention, you will never tire of using it yourself.

Take the picture through an arch, a window, a gate or a branch of an overhanging tree making these serve as a "frame" for your picture. Palm and other subtropical trees are very photogenic for this purpose and the movement of their branches or leaves needs to be "stopped" only partially. The most ordinary shots take on an extraordinary value when you utilize this pictorial device.

When taking such a shot, calculate your exposure not for the lighting available on the "frame" part of the picture but expose for the lighting on the scene beyond it. The frame will, most likely, be in shadow while the scene beyond, the real picture, will probably be in the brightest light.

You can afford to underexpose the less important *frame*. However, if any part of the frame has any interest of its own, a compromise exposure might be indicated. If you can evaluate the *pictorial* values, an exposure meter can settle the *exposure* problems. By its use, it is possible to analyze how far apart are the light values and the necessity to sacrifice one part of the scene for the other.

Even if scenes taken with the "framing" technique have no living creature present, they can still tell a story of some kind. There are story-telling pictures everywhere — wherever there is life, and sometimes where there isn't any. And when story-telling is combined with a travel scene, the picture becomes sure-fire, especially in view of the fact that travel pictures are published more frequently than almost *any other kind of picture*.

Most "live" pictures are best found in the streets, the public squares, the local parks, the corner cafes, along the tiny streams where, most likely, you will see the native women using the "laundermat" that nature supplies. In taking a picture of the last-named scene or similar *genre* subjects, it is best to do so inconspicuously lest offense be given those whose pictures are thus taken without their consent.

In looking for the spectacular, the amateur often overlooks these apparently humdrum scenes right under his nose. If approached with a little imagination, the most ordinary street scene can have extraordinary picture possibilities.

18 *What You Must Know When You Travel With A Camera*

EASY PICTURE-TAKING GUIDE FOR BEGINNERS

The following illustrations and captions furnish a guide for beginners that should enable anyone to make successful pictures from his first roll of film. While specifically aimed at the taking of successful moving pictures, there are points that could easily be adapted to the taking of successful still pictures as well. Continued practice, keeping in mind the principles illustrated, will make a successful photographer in no time at all.

Quick Hints for Better Pictures

19.

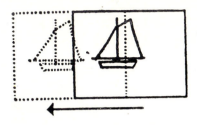

Turn the camera slowly to keep the subject where it should be

Remember: close-ups enliven a picture

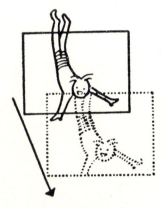

Up or down, be sure to keep subject in center of the finder

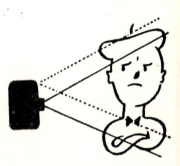

Watch out for parallax. The finder is generally higher than the lens and this must be compensated for on close-ups.

Swing your camera to follow the action of a swiftly-moving object

The average movie scene should take not less than 6 seconds; count off: "twenty-one, twenty-two, etc."

QUICK HINTS FOR BETTER PICTURES

- Get close to your subject. Close-ups, movie or still, are infinitely more dramatic and interesting than long shots. Don't shoot till you see the whites of their eyes. This is suggested not only for still cameras but also for movie work.
- People, children, animals, are more interesting than the most beautiful landscapes unadorned.
- Landscapes can be made more interesting if they include animals or people.
- Side-lighting is more interesting, gives better modeling (roundness) than flat front-lighting.*
- Camera from a high viewpoint *diminishes;*
- Camera from a low viewpoint *exaggerates,* distorts,† makes dramatic.
- Back-lighting, in conjunction with side-lighting, gives best all-round modeling; there should be sufficient front lighting to get some detail in the shadow area facing the camera, unless a semi-silhouette is the desired effect.
- When using back-lighting alone (sun or artificial), a considerable increase in exposure is required, plus an efficient lens shade. If a meter reading is made of a back-lighted subject, get a reading quite close to the subject to avoid the false reading the back-light would **give.**

Photo Samuel E. Lessere

Flower Girl in Baden Baden

*Except when using color, when the safest technique is flat front-lighting.
†Distortion is minimized when using a long focus lens, the usual equipment on the larger cameras.

Quick Hints for Better Pictures 21

- Lens shade is useful under all conditions, even with modern coated lens.
- Over-exposure *flattens* contrast.
  Under-exposure *increases* contrast.
  However, both are dependent on length of development. Either technique is tricky; the beginner, especially anyone who hasn't the development of the film under his own control, had best try for uniformly exposed negatives.
- Do not forget to remove slide from film-holder (on plate back cameras) before shooting.
- Do not forget to pull lens out all the way on collapsible miniature cameras—to the infinity position—before shooting. And be sure to remove lens cap.
- When taking pictures of animals in a zoo (if it is permitted) aim your camera between the bars guarding the animals. The finished print, not showing the bars, will look as though the shot was taken in open country.
- Make a habit of advancing film after every shot.*
- In taking an action picture (with a still camera or a camera not equipped for fast shutter speeds), plan to shoot when the action has slowed or temporarily stopped. A child's swing, for example, reaches a point at top or bottom of the swinging action when even a slow shutter can successfully "stop" action. With a person running or walking, the same success can be had with slow shutters if the picture is taken with the action going towards or moving away from the camera in a direct line. (See section on Action Photography)
- Fast shutter speeds are mandatory when the action is across the line of the camera. Speeds anywhere between 1/200th and 1/1000th of a second are necessary to stop such action, dependent, of course, on the velocity of the action. No table giving shutter speeds for such movement is absolutely to be relied upon though such a table is given in the section on Action Photography.
- When exact architectural detail is desired, hold the camera level with the subject. Tipping the camera in any direction will only distort verticals and horizontals in the subject, even with the longer focal length lenses.†

---

*Except when you know you won't be shooting again for a long time, on cameras with a shutter that's cocked when film is advanced. It's not a very good idea to leave shutters cocked for long periods; the shutter springs, under prolonged tension, can result in impaired shutter action and a repair bill. Few photographers are aware of this fact.
†This does not apply to view cameras or cameras having front and back adjustments; those adjustments can compensate for any distortion, the amount of compensation needed being clearly established on the ground glass back.

22 *What You Must Know When You Travel With A Camera*

Photo Samuel E. Lessere

A Turkish bath in Paris — note the distorted vertical and horizontal perspectives rendered by a miniature camera. Accurate rendering of architecture requires view camera, hence the need for bellows.

- Try not to take several pictures in one (a common failing). Isolate the subject of main interest and take that only, avoiding distracting backgrounds. A picture should have only one center of interest and should include only such objects as will tend to lead the eye to that center.

- When taking a picture of a person in a regional costume, make it a close-up, if you can; that is, if the person will pose for the purpose. The costume itself will often determine whether the picture should be of the bust or the full-length figure. In either case, be close enough to take in just the significant part of the subject. If, however, the background also contributes some significant local color, include as little as necessary for your purpose. Just to be sure you do not clutter up your shot with extraneous detail, it might even be advisable to take a separate shot of the figure alone.

Quick Hints for Better Pictures

- If the subject you want is completely surrounded by distracting objects, the subject can be isolated in two ways: (1) by shooting from a very low viewpoint, which gives only the sky as a background; generally this will involve some distortion especially with short focal-length lenses, but it will be a dramatic kind; (2) by opening the lens wide open (decrease your exposure accordingly), and focusing sharply on the main subject; this will throw surrounding objects out of focus and they will appear as indiscernible blurs in the print. The subject itself should determine which method you should choose. The low viewpoint against sky is always a practical method.

- Don't shoot without walking around your subject and viewing it from several angles. The first viewpoint may not be the best; another angle or viewpoint may be better. If the subject is important, shoot from all angles. Later, you can select the best.

- When you shoot "candid", try to do everything casually, unobtrusively. Try not to attract attention, to "sort of" melt into the background. For a photographer to be noticed is fatal for "candid" work. If you hang around for a fairly long time, people in the vicinity will have a chance to get used to you and then dismiss you from their attention. Then you will have your chance.

- Before taking a candid shot, or any shot in a crowded locality, make sure before shooting that there's nothing nearby that may move into the field of the lens unexpectedly while in the process of shooting. People may stroll right into your path, a bicyclist (Europe has thousands of them) may suddenly appear around the corner, an automobile appear out of nowhere. To wait until all such possibilities are eliminated may require a lot of patience, but it's cheaper to waste time than to waste film, or to lose a precious shot.

- A really graphic shot (as a matter of fact, it's done often) would be a picture of a member of your party in conjunction with a nearby military guardsman. This can more readily be done in tolerant and easy-going Britain than anywhere else. But ask permission anywhere —you have nothing to lose. And you don't need to tip for the privilege. You might (in Monte Carlo anyway) offer a cigarette. Usually a cheerful, friendly thanks is sufficient.

- When using a tree branch or similar object as a "frame," wait till the branch ceases to sway in the wind. Even the slightest movement becomes exaggerated in an object close to the camera and spoils the shot. Or shoot at a high enough shutter speed to stop action on the near object. Many photographers forget to do this when taking a distant still landscape through a moving "frame." And, of course, many do this deliberately for a special effect.

- An extremely low viewpoint—that is, with the camera almost on the ground and pointed up at the subject—has the effect of enlarging the subject, makes the subject dominate to the point of distortion, especially with short focal length lenses. There are subjects and situations that lend themselves to this treatment, as described elsewhere in the book.
- Contrariwise, a high viewpoint—as when the camera points down on a street from a balcony—diminishes the subject, has the effect of miniaturizing it. That technique also has its place in your picture-taking technique.
- When shooting children, it's best to kneel down to approximately their physical level before shooting. Do the same with small animals, pets, etc. However, on occasion, more dramatic pictures of the same subjects may be had by shooting from a level even lower than theirs; this may involve groveling on the ground but no enthusiastic photographer spares himself small inconveniences.
- One picture of an interesting subject can be good; two pictures, from varying viewpoints of the same subject will be better; a series, in logical sequence, is the very best, not only for yourself but for possible sale. In any case, when taking many pictures, it is possible, later, to choose the best single one for enlargement.
- When using flash lighting, be sure to have strong, fresh batteries. Have the batteries tested occasionally and replace them when necessary—they are cheaper than missed pictures and wasted bulbs. Some flash equipment enables the user to test his batteries himself by flashing a small pilot lamp.

Photo Samuel E. Lessere
They make them big in Holland

- Divide a landscape picture in a pleasing proportion between sky and subject—never half and half. Either give approximately 1/3 the space to sky or 1/3 space to landscape, depending on which is of greater interest at the moment. A dramatic effect is often achieved by dividing the space into even greater extremes than the proportions suggested.

- Don't confine your picture-taking to bright sunlight. Some extremely interesting shots can be made on overcast days, in mist, or rain. Try a shot on a rainy day at the precise moment when the sun is beginning to come out and shine through the rain. Be sure to have a lens shade on if the picture is taken looking into the sun. People walking in mist give an effect difficult to achieve in any other way. Such pictures are frequent prize-winners.

- Sometimes it's possible to remove distracting objects in foreground or background. If they cannot be removed, simply choose another location, if possible.

- It is best not to take pictures of people in direct sunlight near midday. The light contrasts caused by sunlight directly overhead are too strong for the film to render the subject as the eye sees it. In fact at any time, when a good portrait is wanted, the best results are obtained in *bright* shade. That kind of lighting furnishes sufficient contrast for good modeling. If direct sunlight is the only light available, an improvised reflector should be used to bounce light into the shadow area of the subject.

- When picturing flowers, don't take a large group, even though it looks good to the eye. It is much more effective to shoot a small cluster. Use the smallest lens opening possible to give the utmost depth of field — close-ups give only a small depth of field (sharp focus).

- When you're engaged in work where you have to act fast (candid, action, etc.)—it's a good idea to set your camera in advance, in a fixed combination of shutter speed, lens opening, and distance scale. Then all you need to do thereafter is to keep at the distance preselected and shoot, without the necessity to stop for setting the camera. Miniature cameras, because of their great depth of field, are ideal for this technique. Many cameras have distinguishing markings (usually in the form of red or green dots) to indicate settings that permit such rapid, automatic action.

- If people stare too fixedly at the camera ("freezing up" is the technical expression), pretend you've taken the picture and, as they relax in relief, shoot them. Or pretend you're not ready to take the picture and engage them in conversation, tell a funny story, etc.; as they relax in response, pull that trigger.

26 *What You Must Know When You Travel With A Camera*

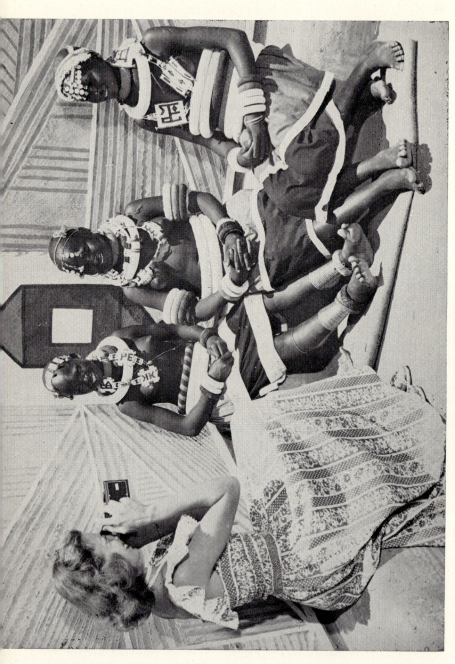

Transvaal, Three Ndebele Girls being photographed by young tourist.

- Watch out for distracting backgrounds. If the person being photographed is standing in front of a tree, your *eye* will separate the two; your camera will not. The finished picture will look as though the tree is growing out of the person's head. A successful photographer is one who learns to see his subject as the camera lens sees it, not as it appears to his eye.

- A picture of older persons is most effective taken in late afternoon with side lighting from a low sun. The side lighting brings out the texture and character of an old face. Low side lighting brings out the texture of any object, with dramatic effect.

- Above all things, relax. A tense attitude does not produce good pictures. A relaxed attitude produces not only better pictures; it's a lot more fun.

KNOW YOUR EQUIPMENT

In order to take full advantage of such picture opportunities that may rise unexpectedly, you should have a thorough knowledge of your equipment so that you can get it into action quickly and without hesitation.

Whether your camera is an inexpensive box camera or the latest super-dooper combined reflex-and-rangefinder 35mm, f/1:5 lens camera (there is one such), you should be thoroughly familiar with its limitations as well as its strong points so you'll know what you can attempt and what you had best leave alone.

As an example, the marvelous 35mm camera mentioned would be a complete failure if you attempted to take with it a picture rendering precise architectural detail from a low viewpoint. The short focal length of the lens would greatly distort the perspective of the vertical lines of the structure.

If you are using a tripod, know how quickly you can get it set up and into action for the pictures you wish to take. Obviously, if it is a nuisance to set up, you can't get into action quickly enough to take advantage of a sudden and unexpected situation.

The same necessity for thorough knowledge occurs when you want quick action with flash equipment, unless that equipment is already mounted on the camera. Indeed, many photographers always keep their flash equipment mounted on the camera for just such emergencies. Thus, it is always ready for what professionals call a "grab" shot.

For similar reasons, many photographers keep their lens filters always handy by mounting them on the camera carrying strap, if the filters have the kind of case that can be snapped onto the strap. Thereby, groping around in one's pockets or in a "carry-all" case for a required filter is eliminated.

If you employ supplementary lenses—most 35 mm cameras make provision for interchangeable lenses for the purpose—you should have a good previous knowledge of what each supplementary lens can do for the particular subject you wish to photograph. Also you should have had a fair amount of practice in the quick changing of such lenses.

If you do know your camera thoroughly, you will never have to hesitate but will be able to shoot with the confidence of a person who knows what he is about and the results he may expect.

Not alone should you know what you may expect from your camera; you should know what you may expect from every other piece of your equipment. Thus you will know what allowances you may have to make in your exposure meter readings for any individual shot. Certain tricky lighting situations need considerable accommodation and compromise. Contrary to general belief, an exposure meter is not an infallible guide but one that needs interpretation for best results.

WOULD YOU LIKE TO MAKE YOUR PICTURES OUTSTANDING PICTURES?

Well — Here Are A Few Hints

Have you ever taken a picture standing on your head? Or lying full-length on your belly on the ground? Sounds crazy, doesn't it? Yet, believe it or not, pictures have been taken that way—and, incidentally, were prize-winners.

Which goes to show that there are almost as many ways to take pictures as there are photographers—and their cameras. Every once in a while, when it is believed that there could not possibly be a new angle for a shot, some eccentric character comes along and finds one.

The important point about such photographic antics to the amateur is that there are more viewpoints and camera angles than just pointing your camera directly at a scene and blazing away. A little advance thinking will suggest the best possible approach to a given subject or, at least, your *individual* way of looking at it. Do not denigrate yourself —your solution to a photographic problem may be just as good as the next man's. Like the Irishman who said he was as good as any other man and a damn sight better.

For example, and just to show what frequent problems are to be encountered, how would you take a picture of a Romanesque cathedral, to do it justice? Or an English cathedral in the Perpendicular style? Or one in the Gothic style, just to add to the complications? Would you take all such pictures in the same manner? If you do, your pictures would be neither outstanding nor dynamic representations of the subjects.

As you may know, Romanesque architecture is generally low and massive and tends to be flat. As a variation there is its Byzantine relative, with rounded decorative domes and gables, seen at their most characteristic in the Venetian San Marco and Florence's famous Baptistery and Duomo. These all cover an amazing lot of ground but do not reach for the sky with slender, lofty spires and flying buttresses to support them as do cathedrals in the Gothic manner.

This is not to declare that one style has any superiority over another. The differences are not qualitative and each style has its own authentic beauty and enthusiastic devotees. But the differences *do* dictate a non-uniform approach to the problem of photographing them.

The massive, low, Romanesque style suggests an eye-level view or even a stance (if that can be arranged) at a bit above street level, as from the second story of a building opposite. And one should try for an oblique or even a right angle view to show the length and size of the structure. If a front view is taken, it should confine itself to the pillared facade; generally, a front view could not begin to show the length of the building.

The Gothic building, on the other hand, suggests a worm's-eye view, so to speak. That is, you can bend low and point the camera upwards to take in the enormous skyward sweep of the spires and the graceful, repetitive motif of the Gothic windows. With short focal length lenses (such as are employed on miniature cameras) there will result a considerable amount of distortion because of the low viewpoint but the distortion actually lends dynamism to the effect.

If closely defined architectural detail is the desideratum, it were best to take pictures of cathedrals in soft, diffused light rather than in brilliant sunshine. The glare of bright sunlight would furnish too much contrast and would tend to wipe out significant detail. But if the flying buttresses, that outstanding characteristic of the Gothic style, appeal, good sunlight will supply dimension and dramatic contrast.

Further, if pictorial, rather than architectural effects are desired, especially when photographing a Gothic structure, wait (if you have time, that is) till a nicely shaped cloud floats in juxtaposition to the top of the structure on which your camera is aimed. Be sure, then, to have at least a medium yellow filter on your lens and increase the exposure to compensate for the filter.* The resulting shot will give you something to be proud of and will be a fillip to your memory of the trip.

An extraordinary added pictorial quality to enhance your picture of a Gothic cathedral could be introduced if you could include in it a subject that resembles the Gothic in appearance or tradition. Here artists have an undeniable advantage, since artists can arrange Nature to suit themselves—and the subject. The trick, at its best, involves a repetition of motif. You might just be fortunate enough to find something to include that will do the trick. If, by chance, some nuns should be passing by, in their high-pointed coifs, that would be just fine. You get the idea?

Interior shots of churches, where permitted, involve other considerations, though some of the principles laid down in the foregoing can

---

*You might also try a shot without increasing exposure for the filter; the negative will be underexposed but the semi-silhouette effect and deep cloud will be dramatic.

Photo Courtesy Danish Tourist Bureau

The Hans Christian Andersen Contest winners photographed in front of Hamlet's world famous castle, Kronborg, at Elsinore, 25 miles north of Copenhagen and dating back to 1574.

also be applied. Each individual photographer will choose, of course, the interior subjects that appeal to him—tastes vary.

Unless armed with color film, stained glass windows should form only a part of the photographic scheme in interiors. If their designs are uncomplicated pictorial motifs, they make interesting photo-drawings, because of the linear qualities. And they are comparatively easy to photograph in black and white film because one can ignore exposing for the dark portions of the interior and concentrate on the light coming through the window only—taking the picture at a slight angle to avoid direct sunlight into the lens. But generally the specific appeal of stained glass is *color*. For that, you will most certainly need a tripod and a long exposure especially if there's no sunlight playing on the windows directly. And you will need permission to use the tripod.

When it comes to detailed photos of door carvings, knockers, or, for example, the world-famous Ghiberti doors on the Florence Baptistery, a close-up, eye-level view is best. These are not subjects to be enhanced by tricky camera angles or made dynamic by unusual approach —if it *is* detail you're after, and sharply defined detail at that. Also, do not, if you value your film, take these subjects in glaring sunlight. They are in sufficient relief in ordinary bright light to give all the modelling you want without exaggeration.

A different effect may be had in late afternoon sunlight, which is much softer. Then you can take pictures of such subjects with the sun playing on the carvings at a sharp, slanting angle. Such slanting lighting serves to highlight the grain of the material being photographed and is especially effective with old, weather-worn wood, marble, or any material of coarse texture.

Museum Interiors

Photos of paintings, statuary, or exhibits in museums are also best at eye-level, for reasons already given. Get as close up as the camera focussing allows to eliminate everything from the view except the painting or object itself. If this is not always possible, you will have to plan to *crop* the negative later when making an enlargement to eliminate all extraneous material from the print. Again, for this kind of picture-taking—in most circumstances—you will need a tripod or fixed support because you'll need to use the smallest lens opening available to get sharp detail and depth. F/22 is adequate.

If your camera is a focussing camera but is not equipped with a rangefinder, you should calculate the distance between camera and subject very carefully because, in a close-up, the depth of sharp focus is very shallow indeed. Often, depending on the camera, the field of sharp focus is to be calculated in inches. Good cameras have a depth-of-focus scale engraved on the lens. This is a great aid in determinining focal values.

With the average fixed-focus box camera, of course, you have no choice; you will simply have to stand off from the subject about 8 feet, unless you have a close-up attachment (available in photo shops as an accessory) to fit over your lens. And of course, too, you should not expect from a box camera the fine definition of detail that may be had with the more expensive lenses.

Bridges Are Pictorial

Bridges in foreign lands are, generally, less functional (which is to say: austere) in appearance than ours. Often they possess a lot of individuality and character, presenting numerous pictorial possibilities—and alternatives. You could take an oblique angle shot from one of the river banks to show the over-all length and structural detail. It's the kind of shot that must not be neglected in the case of the magnificent Ponte Vecchio in lovely Florence. An antique structure, of venerable age, it was, happily, spared in the last war. Bridges in Paris are outstanding.

Alternatively, you could stand at one end of the bridge, place or hold the camera about two feet above the ground and take a long-view picture showing the length of the bridge and its traffic from that low angle. Distorted perspective again, but dynamic and impressive.

Be sure, though, that the view of the camera is not obstructed for the entire length of the structure to the far end. If, however, the bridge curves upwards at the center, the camera will have to be placed so that its view is higher than the center curve and it "sees" to the other end. Because you are attempting to take in both near and far views in such a shot, the lens opening should be as small as practicable.

You might also take a picture of the river beneath, using the supporting pillars or cables as a "frame" for the shot. People walking on or off the bridge at either end would furnish another interesting shot, and the whole would constitute a story series of the bridge scene. That would be taking a leaf out of the picture-news magazine technique.

In river scenes (from bridges) do not concern yourself with stopping the action of the running stream, no matter how turbulent it appears to be. The scene becomes more authentic if some water motion is revealed. There's nothing so deadly from a pictorial standpoint as running water "frozen" in action. Try "freezing" action in pictures of a waterfall sometime to see what I mean.

If small boats are moving about in the camera's field of view, that's another story. Stop movement for them and let the stream go on its merry way; it will then assume much less importance than the boats anyway. This gives a clue to the kind of selective compromises necessary for a discriminating photographer. Flexibility is the word.

Nor do you have to worry about stopping action on pictures of fishermen, as a rule. They have already immobilized themselves. Certainly this is true of fishermen along the French Seine where the reported catch averages one small fish per fisherman per year, if my informant isn't doing a "leg-pull" on me. My own eyes are confirmation.

On some bridges—notably those in the French Provence region—fishermen may be observed pursuing (the word is used euphemistically) their quarry from the bridge itself. In such case, you could combine both sources of pictorial interest in the one shot. They need not necessarily be "grab" (candid) shots, either. Fishermen the world over are avid performers before a camera. Their craftsman pride can be appealed to for posing for just the kind of picture you want.

In your anxiety to get a picture of bridge *and* fisherman, do not neglect to get a *close-up* of the fisherman alone. I said "close-up"— six feet off or even closer, depending on your equipment. The shot doesn't have to be full-length, unless boots and trousers are an integral part of his costume. Often a bust view, but including a view of his equipment, will be adequate.

Take Pictures of the Choo-Choo Trains

There have been hundreds of pictures of foreign trains and railroads, yet their variety and individualistic portrayal are far from exhausted. You should not fail to take a picture of the interior of a foreign train. So different from ours, the train interiors are as picturesque as their antiquated-looking exteriors. Did you ever see, at an American Legion convention, the reproduction of the French military trains (circa 1914), with their marking of "8 Cheval—40 Hommes"? Then you'll know what I mean. Interiors will generally demand flash exposures.

Alas for the picturesque; more modern trains are coming into use constantly. But some of the oldies are still to be seen—that's where your camera comes in. If you can catch a picture with the engineer's head sticking out the window, I don't have to tell you you've got something. If the expression has human interest, you've scored.

On the other hand, when Europe produces modern trains, they're really modern—no fooling! Thus, in Spain, try to catch the famous Talga train running between Madrid and Hendaye. One of the crack trains of Europe, we are just beginning to copy their style in U.S. You may see one on an American railroad by the time this book leaves the printer's hands.

And not to be overlooked, photographically, is the futuristic Milano Rome express in Italy. If you catch that one it will have to be on the fly for it just about takes off, so far as speed is concerned. Best take the picture as a lengthwise shot, then a head-on shot (don't take that too literally), followed by a broadside shot—all while in repose in the station. If you're a train fan, that is—it's an exclusive enthusiasm. But make no mistake about one thing—fan or no fan—such pictures, if they are technically good, are in firm commercial demand.

Try to show passengers at windows; the platform crowds waving farewells (train journeys are of great moment in Europe); the sightseeing glassed-in dome. Don't overlook the conductors. Their uniforms are traditional and supply an interesting contrast to the modernistic decor and structure of the train.

While you're at it take an interior shot of the station itself; that is, those that are still picturesque. Most stations have been rebuilt, due to an unpleasantness of a few years ago—remember?—but there are still a few in existence that may be rewarding. And there are always the Swiss stations.

Station crowds are always interesting. An extraordinary character shot may be obtained by the "grab" technique. If you have fast film and lens, the available light may be sufficient. If not, you may experiment with a time exposure of the station's interior, with a *small* lens opening. Sounds crazy?—what with the moving crowds and all? But just try it. With a small lens opening much movement may not register on the negative at all, strange as that may seem. Anyhow, depending on circumstances, you might just bring off a startling effect—you have only a frame of film to lose.

In Switzerland, in the Dolomite region, in the Tyrolean or French Alps, see if you can use the station platform as a "frame" for the snow-covered mountains in the far view. Be sure part of the station is included in the finder, for contrast and perspective.

Such a picture requires a compromise exposure, since both parts of the subject must register. Underexpose considerably for the station in order not to overexpose the distant mountains bathed in light. Otherwise all that will show in the print will be an expanse of white instead of the scene.

Should you make an enlargement later the under-exposed section (the station) can be "burned in" while holding back the distant view—that's dark room technique. If you do not handle your own technique or if the technique is unfamilar to you, you could instruct the processing laboratory about it, using a tracing of the contact print to indicate the areas to be specially handled.

Monuments — Walled Towns

You may have noticed the emphasis I place on "close-ups". It happens to be an "idée-fixe" on my part. So many amateurs fail to realize how small the negative of the usual hand-held cameras are, especially the miniatures. They are frequently so disappointed when valued subjects are merely pinpointed in the final print—even when enlarged. I have always believed that, with the cameras employed by most persons, they should be as close to the subject as is reasonably possible and eliminate everything else completely.

However, there are situations where close-ups are as difficult to achieve as getting close up to a mother-in-law. Castles perched high up on hills which are steep enough to tax anyone's climbing muscles are cases in point. Take the glory of ancient Greece: the Parthenon; to get a close-up of that magnificent ruin really demands the use of an 8x10 view camera.

Or medieval Carcassonne, with its surrounding walls. In all of these situations a flexible approach is indicated. You can't get the whole thing in one shot—definitely.

You might start with a long shot, taking in some of the surrounding terrain. A medium shot, to take in the entire structure, would follow logically. That might be taken from a low viewpoint to suggest the majestic dominance of the structure over its surroundings and to show its lofty perch and the grandeur of its history.

Castles high above the Rhine call for the same kind of versatile treatment. But, remember that even with long shots a process of selection is still necessary. There are many vantage points and one could easily be superior to another. If you cannot find a completely satisfactory point of vantage, make the best of the situation and see if you cannot then find something to use as a "frame" for the distant shot.

There nearly always are trees to serve this purpose. But because trees are so universally used in this manner, try to find something else to serve. Ingenuity will find something. Once, finding myself in a predicament vis a vis such a situation, I used the pointing hand of a member of my party. All that was shown in the print was the arm and the pointing hand directed to the distant castle across the river. It furnished a neat problem in focal depth but, on a tripod, a tiny lens opening, and a fairly long exposure, the picture came off quite well.

When I showed this picture to a friend, who is in show business, he thought the scheme would be improved by a picture of a ballet dancer's leg kicking skyward and pointing to the distant scene. The trick then is to find the dancer and lose the wife. Anyhow, there are limitless possibilities—roll your own.

Walled towns are best shown in their entirety, in long shots; otherwise they have little meaning. After all, you have to show that the town is walled and showing just a small section of it gives no such indication. However, to carry the story still further, one should show a close-up view of the town gate, generally an integral part of walled towns.

Such a modern city as Paris, incidentally, still has a vestige of such an entrance gate; you can easily find out where it is. The caption would have to explain that it's part of the old city gate because it has small resemblance now to its original appearance. Except for the fact that they are no longer attached to walls, some of the English arched gates quite plainly reveal their original function.

Spain abounds still in walled towns, as does Italy. And, with regard to medieval appearance, an interesting old town rarely visited by tourists, is Piacenza, east of Milan. Its streets show little change from their ancient appearance. But then everybody has his favorite medieval town in Europe.

Views of Florence, from the nearby perch of Fiesole, afford fine distant shots, not only of Florence itself in the valley below, but distant views of typical Italian landscapes. You'll need clear skies and nice sunshine to give sparkle to the views from Fiesole of the Baptistery, the Campanile, and the Duomo.

In Milan, you can get access to the top of its Duomo (second largest church in Europe, after St. Peter's, in Rome). From the top of this structure, you can get an intriguing view—and photographs—of the historic square below. Point the camera straight downwards for one shot, and at a more gradual slant for another. Also get one of the rest of the city from that height, excluding the Square.

If you visit the chateaux region of France, in season, you might take the night trip to one or more of the famous ones. Schedules of these trips are to be had at dozens of travel agencies of Paris. At night, these flamboyant French castles are illuminated; this lends considerable enchantment to the old structures. When using the illumination, you might try straight snapshots, with fast film, or tripod work with slow film or color. The guides, no photographers themselves, but out of their experience with photographer-tourists, can give you pretty accurate advice about exposures.

The Grand Place (in Brussels) which has been termed, deservedly, the most medieval single sight in Europe, offers no single vantage point from which to picture the square in its entirety, unless you engage a helicopter. You will need to take several isolated long shots of the famous rectangle. But do not neglect to take, in addition, close-ups of individual subjects of appeal. They'll be all around you. Some of them will be walking.

Picturesque Canals

When God made Europe, he made the canals first. After which, refreshed by the view of what He created, He tackled the rest of the job. This is my own inspired interpretation of Holy Writ but you don't have to take it on faith—have a look for yourself.

Copenhagen, Amsterdam, Bruges, Annecy, Italy's Grand Canal in Venice, and many others not even listed in guide books. You'll fall all over but not, let's hope, *into* them. And they're all made to order to consume photo film.

Of course, in Amsterdam, you'll take the very inexpensive boat trip through the canals. It gives vantage points as no sightseeing bus trip could. And what photographic opportunities—it's enough to make one's camera eye water.

Throw caution to the winds—just bang away. A blind man couldn't fail to get interesting pictures. Don't neglect to take a close-up of the boat's lecture guide in the process of pointing to some interesting sight. Here would be a fine opportunity of trying the trick of combining a pointing hand with a picturesque subject.

You can get a picture of the guide in full as foreground; then, later, crop away all but the hand as it points . . . If the guide looks like an interesting character, leave him in full portrayal. Or have both. You pays your money.

In Venice, on the Grand Canal, pictures of gondolas have been done in such variety that it seems impossible to get a new slant on the subject. But don't let that stop you. You might still want your own version and you might just come up with a novel shot. That's one of the fascinations of photography; unique achievement may lie just around the corner—the canal corner, that is. No one has yet succeeded in photographing the Canal's smells—perhaps because no one has tried, or wanted to.

Tricky Interior Exposures

In suggesting the picture possibilities in museum and church interiors, there must not be overlooked that these interiors represent exposure problems. Where the available light is fairly strong and you are equipped with lens openings of f/3.5 and fast film, you can probably get away with 1/25 second exposure.

But with color film or black and white whose ASA speed is below 50, you will need a tripod and a longer exposure. That means a time exposure. I would suggest that, with time exposures, you experiment with two separate exposures—one to be double the other. But with the more expensive color film, there would naturally be a reluctance to indulge in such an extravagance.

If the interior is fairly dark with no substantial window area to relieve the darkness, you might use 4 seconds at f/5.6, using the new fast Ektachrome Daylight film. As long as the camera is on a tripod—as it would have to be with such an exposure—you might halve this exposure, i.e. about 8 seconds at f/8. If very dark interior (in which case color work seems dubious) but there still is something you can't resist, use 12 seconds at the 5.6 lens opening.

If exposures like these are indicated and you do not have a tripod, do not despair; you can still manage. There will nearly always be available a bench or wall shelf on which you can place the camera and from which you can take the shot. Of necessity, you will have to use a cable release to avoid jarring the camera. Sometimes you might even find valuable an extension cable release, several feet long, which you can operate from a distance.

Outstanding Pictures 39

Stained glass windows do not require such lengthy exposures but they still might require exposures longer than should be hand-held. Especially since it may be desirable that they be taken without direct sunlight coming through them. They are best taken that way—with only the natural daylight coming through. Here the precise exposure is determined by the nature of the design on the glass. If there is much clear area in the glass, more light is available and less exposure needed. If, on the other hand, there is a lot of closely integrated design, impeding outside light, longer exposures are necessary.

Exposure meters are not a great help in such situations; only experiment and experience, or a fat pocketbook, for wasted film, will suffice. I can only say that anyone who has seen some of Europe's beautiful stained glass will not let film cost deter him from trying to record them for his future pleasure.

Incidentally, if for any reason you failed to get a picture you later on find you really want (you could run out of film at the crucial moment, you might reach a photogenic spot at night, or you might just have neglected to take a picture), then you'll want to know about the library of one million travel pictures, neatly divided into almost 16,000 subjects, which Meston's Travels, Inc. can supply in the form of color slides. Its catalog costs 35c, and it's located at 3801-H North Piedras, El Paso, Texas.

ACTION PHOTOGRAPHY

— from Airplane, Train, Bus, Auto, Ship, etc.

It would seem that action photography might have no reason for inclusion in a book on travel photography and, instead, might well be reserved for treatment in a conventional photographic textbook. However, the tourist is precisely the person who most often finds himself moving at varying rates of speed, in public conveyances, just when the most interesting objects for photography present themselves.

Of course, such opportunities for striking photographs must not be lost even though they demand photography involving movement on the part of the photographic objects, or the photographer, or of both simultaneously.

There's no use pretending that photography practiced under moving conditions is easy; it is the very reverse. Nevertheless, some fundamental rules, based on experience and technical factors, can be laid down for the guidance of the tourist to help him achieve as much success as may be possible for him in this difficult field.

To take successful pictures from a moving position, three essentials must be observed: One must be able to judge approximately the speed of the movement of the object being photographed in relation to one's own movement (if that too is involved); the camera must be preset with all the necessary adjustments of focusing, shutter speed, and lens stop; and one must have calm nerves and steadiness of position, regardless of whether that position is in motion or not. The rest is practice and experience.

While, essentially, taking pictures from train, plane, auto, bus, ship, and auto presents problems similar in *kind,* each means of transportation differs so much from the others as to present problems different in *degree;* each therefore imposes a different approach and a varying technique.

However, one basic principle common to all action photography, apart from the three essentials above noted, may be laid down at the outset. There is considerably less movement, and consequently fewer problems involved, in taking pictures with the movement coming towards or going away from the camera on a direct line or an oblique angle than when the movement crosses your lens at right angles. A glance at the illustrations will make this clear.

Action Photography

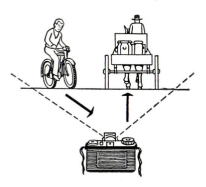
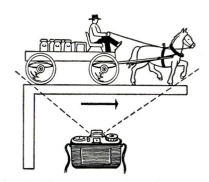

A—Movement on direct line or oblique angle to camera is less rapid

B—Movement at right angle to camera is most rapid

Because of the slower movement of objects at an oblique angle, slower shutter speeds may be employed; because of the swifter movement of objects at right angles to the camera, the highest shutter speeds must be used.

Shutter speed is not the only problem involved. When an object is coming towards the camera on a direct line or an oblique angle, it is also less difficult to judge the precise instant for snapping the shutter; you are going to get the picture just the same, if you do misjudge the precise moment, even though the focus may be a little inexact or though the object may be a little smaller or larger in the negative than you had intended.

But the case is different when you take a picture of a moving object at right angles to the lens. Then you must judge the exact instant to snap the picture or, very likely, you will find you have no picture at all.

It is this difficulty in taking pictures of extreme movement which has accounted, in part, for the one-time popularity of a special camera (the Robot), which is capable of taking eight pictures a second. With this camera, because of a special built-in automatic mechanism, it is possible to start shooting before the action crosses the camera and the mechanism will keep on shooting until the action has gone past the camera. In this way one is assured of a series of pictures out of which one is almost certain to get just the shot one desires or even a set of pictures in sequence. A movie camera, of course, can be utilized in the same way.

When the Robot was first introduced to the photographic field some years ago, many professionals tried it out and secured highly successful results, though the camera has some limitations; small negative size (24 x 24 mm) being the most serious. More recently, for the same purpose of securing a series of shots quickly, a leading miniature camera maker has supplied an accessory that enables the user to pump several shots per second; the process is not quite so effective as with the Robot, however.

Most of the leading cameras provide what is known as a sports finder, in addition to the regular finder, to enable the photographer to follow movement more easily than is possible with the use of the regular finder on the camera. The most commonly used type of sports finder consists of slots cut into metal rectangles mounted on the camera and aligned in such a way as to permit the user to hold the camera close against his eye while viewing the object and to swing his body and camera to accord with the movement of the object in motion.

Pictures From An Airplane

Airplanes travel in a world that, for all practical purposes, is a new one. It is a world far from the ken of the average land-bound mortal. It is a world in which the most ordinary, most prosaic landscapes take on a new beauty and interest, while landscapes that are beautiful when viewed on land are transformed, from the air, into fairylands of enchantment.

Naturally, the photographic possibilities that lie in such magical transformations have intrigued both amateur and professional photographers ever since the field was open to them and they have risen to the opportunities to create a new world of photographic achievement.

The equipment used by professional photographers for aerial pictures is specialized and elaborate and is beyond both the means and the necessities of the average tourist. Happily, successful aerial pictures can be taken even with an ordinary camera and adequate aerial pictures have even been taken with a box camera. However, it would be naive to expect results from such a camera as a regular thing.

It is recommended that one should have a camera providing shutter speeds up to 1/200 second; 1/400 second would be an even greater assurance of success. Cameras with such shutter speeds generally are also equipped with the quality of lenses suitable for aerial photography.

Pictures in color, with the color film available (Ektachrome, Kodachrome, Kodacolor) give beautiful results. The contrast provided by the natural color of a scene gives all the modeling and depth necessary so one can be less concerned with angles and shadows. The only limitation is the amount of natural light available and the exposures necessary to render a scene correctly.

Needless to say, aerial shots in color supply the last word in accurate and beautiful rendering of the world's enchantment seen from high viewpoints. However, black and white film not only gives fine rendering of aerial views too but its use is often made necessary by the additional speed it makes available in the form of fast panchromatic film. However, color film emulsions are available that almost rival black and white film in speed.

In the taking of aerial pictures a factor that must be given considerable weight is the presence of haze in the atmosphere, of which a certain amount is always present even if not always discernible to the unpracticed eye. The effect of haze, which serves to cast a veil of varying density over the picture, increases with the distance being photographed. To overcome its effect it is desirable and often necessary to use a haze filter, both for color film and for black and white. When using color film, uncorrected haze produces an undesirable bluish cast, and when using black and white film haze causes a considerable reduction in overall contrast and loss of definition in the more distant vistas.

Filtering in Aerial Photography

For color film, Kodak Skylight Filter is recommended and for black and white film, yellow or red filters should be used, depending on the amount of haze present at the time of photographing. To compensate for the loss of light transmission produced by the use of the filters with black and white film, additional exposures must be given, the amount of the additional exposure being dependent on the depth of the coloring in the filter used. When purchasing the filters, you will find out the "factor number," which means the amount of additional exposure necessary for the filter being used.

When using Daylight Type color film with the Skylight Filter, no additional exposure is necessary to compensate for the use of the filter. However, it must be noted that, for aerial photography, color film should be given somewhat more exposure than the film requires for photography on land.

The Camera Must Be Steady

The most important thing to contend with in aerial photography is unsteadiness of the camera, which is really unsteadiness in the photographer. Many professionals weight their cameras, especially if the cameras are light ones. They will attach 6-10 pounds of weight to a 4x5 camera. For smaller cameras it is the practice to form into handles two ends of a 2x4, fasten the camera to the center and attach a cable release to one of the ends, securing the whole with a weight for additional stability.

It is doubtful whether the average tourist will go to such trouble but these details are mentioned because they will throw light on the problems involved. Most tourists dispense with such details (whether they are aware of their advisability or not) and yet have been able to secure quite satisfactory pictures nonetheless.

Shooting From Airliners

The average tourist will have to confine his aerial shooting to passenger airliners. That means he will mostly have to shoot through glass or plastic windows. The camera will have to be held as close as possible to the window without touching it, to avoid undesirable reflections from other windows in the plane. A lens shade may be of some value in this connection; the side curtains may also be used to reduce reflections from the interior.

If the window is slightly dirty, it will not affect the picture, though it might be useful to remove as much dirt or dust as one can. Naturally, that can only be done on the inside of the window.

No part of one's body supporting the camera should be in contact with the body structure of the plane; the idea is to reduce to a minimum the possibility of the plane's vibration being communicated to the camera itself. If a pillow helps to cushion or support one's elbows, it could be used since it helps to insulate the body against some of the vibration.

The best position for photography is in the rear, away from the wing. The shady side of the plane is desirable because the effect of haze is lessened and because direct sunlight on the window would magnify the effects of scratches, dirt and flaws in the window.

The plane's personnel can advise which will be the shady side during the flight. Generally when flying east, it is the left side; and when flying west, the right side.

It would be expedient to cultivate the plane personnel in any case because they can be and often desire to be helpful in matters of this kind. They know their routes perfectly and can often suggest photographic possibilities well in advance of the plane's arrival on the spot so you can be prepared. Pilots have been known to shift the plane's course slightly when that has been of advantage to a photographer. Incidentally, they can also advise what military sites it is forbidden to photograph. Forbidden areas are not always recognizable at cruising altitudes.

The tourist may also desire to take shots of the interior of the plane or of some of the passengers whose acquaintance has been made. For this purpose you may use your exposure meter* in the ordinary way or, lacking one, calculate the exposure as you would for a picture on the ground in deep shade. It might be advantageous to wait till the plane passes or goes through some low-flying clouds which, by reflecting sunlight into the interior of the plane, will supply greater illumination.

In any case, for interior shots, use a slightly faster shutter speed than you would on the ground (opening up your lens in accordance) to overcome the plane's vibration as it affects the steadiness of the camera. Fair results may be obtained with an exposure of 1/50 second at f/8, using Kodak Tri-X film.

Many tourists get great satisfaction from making a photographic story series of the entire plane trip. You can begin such a series by taking shots of the airport; its signal towers (these can be very effective by shooting against a sky darkened by proper filters); the attendants loading baggage; the maintenance crew at work on the plane;

For regular external aerial shots, an exposure meter is of small value; the readings will be fallacious and, if followed, will result in underexposure.

crowds at the airport to greet passengers; passengers boarding the plane; plane personnel; the warm-up; the take-off; pictures of planes passing on their way in or out; fellow-passengers; scenes in actual flight; and, finally, similar shots on arrival at the plane's destination. Still cameras skillfully operated, can obtain such a series successfully—movie cameras require less skill to obtain a vivid series that will be long cherished.

Because of the long vistas generally photographed from the plane in flight, there should be some attempt to give *scale* to the picture, to give perspective, some idea of size and distance. The conventional scheme is to include the plane's wing-tip in a corner of the shot. In any case, it is advantageous to have an important center of interest: a distant tower, a nearby hill, some farm building, a bridge; anything which, by known contrast, gives scale to the rest of the picture.

Shutter Speeds and Focusing

When shooting from the plane in flight, focusing is no problem. The camera is set at *infinity* and kept there. Shutter speeds may vary from 1/100 second to 1/400 second. While there are cameras providing higher shutter speeds (1/500 second to 1/1000 second and more), such speeds are rarely necessary for most aerial shooting.

The lower shutter speeds can be used at the higher, cruising altitudes while the higher shutter speeds are required at lower altitudes or before landing, for obvious reasons. When approaching or leaving airports, 1/200 second or faster is required. Once under way, at the higher cruising altitudes, 1/100 second is generally sufficient. Plane vibration and bumpy air are the things to guard against; under such conditions, use your higher shutter speeds — that is, if you take pictures at all; your mind may be occupied with other things then, most likely.

It may be worth noting that the morning hours, especially in summer, provide the smoothest flying weather, though that is the period when haze filters are most necessary too.

Aerial Movies

A movie camera offers some tremendous advantages in aerial shooting, apart from the fluidity it imparts to the scenes being photographed. The most important advantage is the possibility to operate the camera at its higher shutter speeds (32 or 64 frames per second) because these speeds slow up the action being taken and do much to cancel out the bumpiness of the air, the vibration of the plane and any other jerkiness that may be manifested. The higher frame speeds are especially valuable when landing or taking off and at low altitudes when the ground movement is so much swifter than at cruising altitudes.

Do not swing the camera; do not "pan", in other words. Just let the action flow past your camera in the natural way — the result will be the same as though you were panning anyway, so you must not do anything to increase the velocity of movement by your own movements. As with still camera shots, the inclusion of a wing-tip in a corner of the picture will add effectiveness since its stability will give added contrast to the velocity of the ground movement.

Movie film will be greatly enhanced, as with still shots, by the use of Kodak Skylight Filter for color film and the use of yellow or red filters for black and white Panchromatic film. For the latter, the Kodak CK-3 filter is very useful.

Movies of the interior of the plane may not be too successful, the light being generally insufficient for good results, especially when color film is employed. However, if the tourist is anxious for such pictures he might attempt them when flying through bright low-flying clouds. If using black and white film, the new Tri-X had best be employed.

Pictures Taken on or From a Moving Ship

Pictures taken on board ship furnish no problems differing to any extent from those taken on land. Naturally, you will not attempt, will probably not be in the mood to attempt, to take pictures while plowing through stormy seas. At other times, while the ship will contribute some vibration, it will be considerably less than the vibration of a plane. Moreover, since the subjects being photographed on board the ship are subject to the same vibration as is the camera in your hand there is a tendency for the vibration to cancel out. Nevertheless, it is good practice to use the higher shutter speeds you may have available — not less than 1/50 second and 1/100 second would be better.

The same precautions that were suggested with regard to pictures taken from a plane when landing or taking off, apply to pictures taken from a ship of land objects when coming in or going out of a port. Shutter speeds should be increased to allow for the additional movement. Of course, the speed of a ship, under such circumstances, is much less than that of a plane, so the shutter speeds need not be excessive.

The shutter speeds are also determined by the camera angle, a matter which is treated in some detail elsewhere. When the movement is on a direct line with the camera or slightly oblique, 1/100 second is ample. When the movement is at right angles to the camera, the shutter speed should be increased to 1/200 second. That is, providing the only movement is that of the ship moving in or out. When the subjects being photographed are also in action, these shutter speeds should be doubled, lens stops being adjusted accordingly in relation to the available light.

Photographing From a Bus

The tourist may desire to make a complete photographic record of a bus trip just as he might do with a plane trip. Some of the conducted bus trips abroad are quite elaborate affairs and may last through several days.

There is time, generally, to get acquainted with and also to get on intimate terms with fellow-passengers and you will want to take many record shots of them engaged, like yourself, in the numerous sightseeing activities. You may want pictures showing the baggage being loaded on top of the bus (the usual arrangement in Europe), the passengers getting on, a close-up of the hostess and driver, a shot of the bus leaving the station (taken from inside the bus), shots of places passed enroute, of stop-over points, etc. You might also include an over-all picture of the bus itself. And you might take one with the bus personnel posed against it and another with all the passengers lined up outside it. The latter may be a very conventional shot but it is indispensable for record purposes. You may be assured you will have to do your share of posing for such shots taken by the other passengers.

There may actually be more vibration inside a bus than inside a plane depending on the condition of the bus and the roads it traverses. Therefore, for shots taken from inside a bus while in motion, it is advisable to use not less than 1/100 second shutter speed and, if your film and lens speed combination is fast enough, 1/200 second would be better. Unlike on a plane, if the window of the bus is dirty you have the possibility to open it—if you are a young Hercules. If you cannot flex your muscles so effectively, the driver might be glad to oblige.

If, for some reason, it is not expedient to open the window you can shoot through it, just as you were compelled to do on the plane. If, as in the plane, there is a little dirt on the window, the picture will not be noticeably affected. However, if you are a perfectionist, it is possible to clean the inside of the window and, when the bus makes a stop, you can also clean the outside or ask that it be done.

Pictures From a Train

The technique of taking pictures from a train does not differ greatly from that for taking pictures from a bus. Do not let your camera touch the window but keep fairly close to the window when shooting. Guard, as best you can, from communicating the vibration of the train's movement to the camera while shooting.

The long windows in the outside corridors of the old-fashioned trains on the European continent afford the opportunity to take pictures from an oblique angle which is so much easier than taking them at right angles to the camera, as previously explained. At the same time, the long advance views these long corridor windows provide give ample time for preparation for the scenic shots you may wish to take.

These corridor windows are easy to open (unlike bus windows above mentioned) and thereby you have an opportunity to take pictures unhampered by window glass, dirty or not. Since, however, you can never precisely anticipate what reflections might bounce into your lens, be sure to have a lens shade in use always.

During train stops, especially at small villages, there are afforded many opportunities for quaint pictures, uncomplicated by train movement; also pictures of the local station vendors of one kind or another. Frequently, these local vendors wear picturesque indigenous costumes which are interesting in themselves and which furnish so much of the fascination of travel in foreign lands.

Be sure to include a picture of the official on the platform as he gives the signal for the train to depart. These signals, the gestures that accompany them, and the kind of officials who give them vary from country to country, even from village to village, and they are extremely interesting. Since, generally, the signals are given in slow motion, it is easy enough to stop the action with slow shutter speeds.

Take such a picture from a low viewpoint, on a bent knee for example; this lends drama to the shot and makes a towering figure of the signaling official. Of course, if taken from the loading platform outside the train (the best place), this means you have to scramble back onto the train quickly lest you be left behind. I have never had such ill luck but it need only happen once to be disastrous. I doubt that the train would go off without you, though. The signaling official would see to that, I'm sure.

Another interesting picture would be one of the conductor as he examines or takes up passengers' tickets. If you can speak his language, ask him to hold still in the proper pose while you shoot him. More likely than not, he will be amused and be glad to comply. You might promise him a print, if there is any possibility that you could make good on the promise.

Pictures From an Auto

If it is your own car, or one hired by you, your picture-taking conditions are at your own control. They can be taken while in motion (in which case the technique will be the same as that described for bus travel) or they can be taken while stopping at any particular place. In the latter case, the ordinary picture-taking technique on the ground applies and you have no problems.

You might want a picture to show it was taken from a car; in that case, show a part of the windshield in a corner of the shot as foreground. If you are parked on some high point looking across at some long mountain or valley vista, you might include a part of the car in the shot, to give scale to the scene. To include a near object (like the car) in a distant view requires extreme depth of focus, so it will be necessary to stop the lens down to f/16 or even f/22 combined with a slow shutter speed, to give sufficient exposure.

If no object is in motion, you can use 1/25 second safely enough if you have a steady hand; persons with solid nerves have held a camera steady at exposures of one full second — however, I wouldn't guarantee results with such long-held exposures.

Technical Data for Guidance in Taking Action Shots

The following tables are for general guidance only. While they are basic, they cannot pretend to cover all situations. The beginning photographer will find them valuable for most subjects. The advanced or professional photographer will have had enough experience to use the table as a basis for departure. In general, it may be said that, if these rules are followed, one will achieve moderate success and few failures. For outstanding success, nothing quite takes the place of practical experience — outstanding news photographers, for example, don't get that way in a single day.

BASIC SHUTTER SPEEDS FOR SHOOTING MOVING OBJECTS*

On direct line with camera or slight oblique angle	At sharp oblique angle	At right angle
Pedestrians 1/50	Pedestrians 1/100	Pedestrians 1/150
General street movement ...1/100	General street movement ..1/200	General street activity 1/250
Slow vehicles ..1/150	Slow vehicles ..1/250	Slow vehicles ..1/400
People running or bicyclists .1/200	People running or cyclists ..1/300	People running or cyclists ..1/500
Fast vehicles ..1/250	Fast vehicles ..1/400	Fast vehicles .1/1000

Note that the table is for shutter speeds only. Lens stops must be calculated for the amount of light available, and the shutter speed you are compelled to use, to stop the action. Naturally, for action photography, regardless of the speed of the lens you have, you should use the fastest film you can get. The news photographer, using sheet film, has a jump on the amateur in this respect because there is available now sheet film with the amazing ASA speed rating of 1000. The best the amateur can do is to get the Tri-X rollfilm with ASA rating of 400. If, however, the amateur does his own processing, he can increase the effective speed of the film by utilizing some of the strong developers now available.

As to color film, he must be an expert indeed who will attempt action photography with the fastest color film presently available; that is, speaking of still camera work. Movie work is another matter altogether.

50 *What You Must Know When You Travel With A Camera*

At any distance from the camera, the shutter speeds above given can be halved if you have recourse to a trick for taking action shots known as "panning." With this technique, you get the subject located in your sports finder and swing your camera with the moving object, keeping it centered in your sports finder, as you shoot.

When using this technique, the background becomes a complete blur, but the effect is to make the moving object being photographed almost a stationary object. Actually, the blurred background serves to enhance the feeling of speed you wish to impart.

TECHNICAL DATA FOR ACTION PHOTOGRAPHY

Lens Settings for new fast color Film
(Daylight type, 8 or 16 mm)
For average subject* at 16 frames per second**

Altitude	Bright Sun	Hazy Sun	Cloudy bright (below clouds)	Cloudy dull (below clouds)
below 2000 ft.	f/11	f/8	f/5.6	f/3.5
2000 ft. to 4000 ft.	f/11-16	No exposure compensation for altitude necessary on hazy or cloudy days. Do not make color movies, when haze or smoke makes it difficult to see the ground from the plane		
4000 ft. and up	f/16			

— Courtesy Eastman Kodak Co.

* *For deserts, beaches, high obliques including horizon, or snow-covered landscapes, use ½ lens stop smaller. For clouds photographed from above, use 1 stop smaller than for average subjects below 2000 feet.*
** *At 32 frames per second use next larger lens opening.*
At 64 frames per second use next 2 lens stops larger.

Slowest Recommended Shutter Speeds for Aerial Photography
Verticals or low obliques*

Altitude (ft.)	GROUND SPEED in miles per hour				
	75	100	125	150	200
4000	1/50	1/50	1/50	1/50	1/100
3500	1/50	1/50	1/50	1/100	1/100
3000	1/50	1/50	1/100	1/100	1/100
2500	1/50	1/100	1/100	1/100	1/200
2000	1/100	1/100	1/100	1/100	1/200
1500	1/100	1/100	1/200	1/200	1/200
1000	1/200	1/200	1/200	1/400	1/400
500	1/400	1/400	1/400	—	—

—Courtesy Eastman Kodak Co.

* *Taking pictures obliquely as the airplane approaches or leaves the subject may permit slower shutter speeds, providing the slower shutter speed is adequate to counteract camera movement caused by rough air, airplane vibration, etc.*

THE SEQUENTIAL PICTURE STORY

Of the millions of amateur photographers scattered around the world, only a relative handful have progressed beyond the stage of elementary snapshooting. The average tourist-photographer contents himself with shooting one frame of a scene and then, like the legendary Arab, steals away. His day's, or hour's, work is done.

But is it?

Have you ever given thought to how much more satisfactory is sequential shooting of a scene or event? That is to say, a series of shots planned in logical order to give a record of the scene in depth, so to speak.

Let us say you are engaged in a visit to the home of a famous but now dead poet, author, or statesman. The average, thoughtless photographer takes a snapshot of the outside of the historical house. Methodically (because he is something less than a complete idiot) he transcribes in his note-book: "Home of Monsieur X—famous novelist".

If he has some imagination, he even includes in the shot the plaque outside the door which gives the bare facts surrounding the personality.

But the rising and deserved popularity of the great picture-news magazines of the world (there are many outstanding ones in foreign countries, too, incidentally) has triggered amateur photography into emulation of the news series technique.

I use the word "technique" advisedly. Actually, the matter has less to do with pure photographic technique than with story-telling imagination and creativeness. The big-league photographers possess no monopoly of these valued qualities. No amateur need be afraid to compete.

What Does the Story-Telling Technique Demand?

Simply a little forethought and imagination. And a plan. Let us take a hypothetical case and see where it leads us.

Let us say we are visiting the birthplace and early home of the French actress who has established a legend in the theatre of France: Sarah Bernhardt—the Divine Sarah, as she has been termed.

As we enter the village of her birth, we note how little it seems to have been changed by modern ways; we note its rusticity and its quaint 18th Century atmosphere. Wherefore, we select a section of the village (most likely it will be the main "place") and get a shot to establish that atmosphere. We make sure to show the antique-looking, faded Hotel de Ville (City Hall) and the dingy outdoor cafes which, in France, are always found in that important section of the village. All of this will represent the kind of milieu which was the early background of the famous actress.

To round out that picture, we also take one or two shots of local inhabitants in their austere work-a-day clothes and activities.

At the house itself, we take a long shot of the house, including part of the neighbor houses on each side. This is taken at eye-level, to get as much undistorted detail as possible. We also try to get on some nearby height to take a shot looking down on the roofs of the houses to show the contiguity of habitations of villages of this vintage in France.

One of the members of our party will obligingly pose in front of the historical plaque on the gate, going through the motions of studying the plaque or pointing at it for the edification of the rest of the party.

Inside the house, we find an ancient desk, filled with all the fussy bric a brac which is such an integral part of French decor. On the desk we place a child portrait of the French actress (which the custodian has been nice enough to dig up for us) and we take a shot of the desk with the portrait. We take the shot on a tripod, with a tiny lens opening and a long exposure, for utmost fidelity and depth of field.

Next we take a picture of the custodian and his wife (who, presumably, live in the place) and, still on the tripod, we open our lens a bit and take a shorter exposure. People cannot remain immobile as long as inanimate objects.

Following this, we are shown a picture of the actress as a pupil in secondary school, costumed in the cute pinafore all French school children wear. We dig up some old school books and place them on the mantelpiece with the child portrait and include both in our next shot.

Then we are brought to a closet full of the dresses worn by the divine Sarah when already a budding dramatic luminary. Spreading these out as much as possible, to show as many as we can, we train an electric bulb on the closet opening for light and shoot that picture.

One of the ladies of our party hurriedly dons one of the dresses (behind a screen, of course) and we take that shot to show how a modern American young lady would look in a costume of that period. Very charming, too.

Are we through? Not yet. We have to take pictures, interestingly arranged, of some of the old theatre programs and of the billboards, with their bizarre-looking (to our modern eyes) old French poster types, lettering and illustrations.

Nor do we overlook taking a picture of a page from Sarah Bernhardt's diary, with its yellowed paper, the discursive and quaint French script, and the crushed flower in the corner. This is a copying job; we make sure that the camera is trained on the page at an accurate right angle, close the lens down to its smallest opening, and take two time exposures—one doubling the other. We want to make sure that the stains and fading of age are fully registered on the negative for future enlargements. When doing linear work of this kind, it is scarcely possible to overexpose.

A bearded, majestic-looking old man, with his close-fitting beret looking like a Hebrew prophet's skull-cap, has been following us around during all these activities and the custodian stops to explain that the old man, as a boy, knew Sarah quite well. Which goes to explain his intense interest in what we were doing.

So, to round off our hegira, we take a characterful shot of him, stand him a cognac at the adjoining cafe, and we're off to our pension to wind up proceedings by notes in our book. That way we can set down the significant events of the day while they are still fresh in our memory and the remarks will amplify the pictures we have taken.

A year later, these shots and notes will bring back to memory the events of the day and place as vividly as we experienced them, thus making the trip a lifetime investment in travel satisfaction. Voila! Go thou and do likewise!

FLASH PHOTOGRAPHY IS A CINCH

The development of flash photography has removed all the limitations that formerly handicapped the photographer, amateur or professional. Today, when nearly all cameras above the box level are synchronized for flash use (and even many box cameras have built-in provision for flash use), any photographer can take almost any subject, anywhere, any time. And thus a whole new photographic world is opened up. Not only is this true for the stay-at-home photographer; it is doubly true for the traveler.

The traveler will find indispensable use for a flash even before he lands in a foreign country. If you go by ship, there will be hundreds of photographic opportunities during the course of the voyage in which only flash techniques will get the pictures.

There are the ship's parties; the dances; the usual dummy horse races (shoot the expressions of excitement and suspense); the captain's dinner (a gala affair usually scheduled the next to last night of the voyage—be sure to get a picture of the captain; your only chance); groups around the bar, in the swimming pool, even the passengers lined up for the fire-drill.

If you travel by freighter where matters are conducted on a less formal basis so far as the run of the ship is concerned, you can get pictures of the officer on the bridge, the radio operator's room, the galley ("kitchen" to landlubbers), the engine room, freight loading at one of the ports, etc.

While the opportunities on a plane are more limited (see, however, the section on "Action Photography" from a plane, elsewhere), there do exist picture possibilities inside the plane in which flash may be either the sole source of light or function as a supplement to the available daylight which may often be insufficient for the fast exposure made necessary by plane movement.

Flash photography may be an essential requirement once you land too. Many places you'll be visiting are indoors where the available light just won't be enough for a well-exposed picture.

Even outdoors, there will be overcast days (weather is as unpredictable abroad as at home, and picture opportunities do not wait on the weather—the average tourist just doesn't have the time to wait around. If he doesn't shoot when the picture is there, in nine cases out of ten, it's a picture he'll never get.

So if the light is too poor for the definition you want, use flash and get the shot. In very poor light let the flash determine the exposure. If the light is not too poor but just doesn't supply the contrast to give sparkle, expose for the flash as a supplementary, "fill-in" source of light. Or arrive at a compromise between the two. Experience is the best teacher in this matter.

In so far as flash equipment is concerned, battery flash equipment for small bulbs (some of the equipment is less than half the size of a cigarette package), particularly the new B-C variety of equipment, reduces the weight and bulk to the point where the equipment is no burden at all. Some of these bulb-exciters make use of the new tiny hearing-aid batteries, and fit neatly in the palm of one's hand, apart from the reflectors. Altogether, the combined equipment may weigh as little as 10 ounces.

B-C equipment has more than a weight advantage over the older type of equipment. In the old style flash, current worked directly from the batteries to the bulb and the current was restricted to the internal resistance of the dry cells. In B-C flash there is a capacitor (B-C stands for "battery-capacitor") which stores up energy between flashes, and when you shoot there is an unrestricted flow of current from the *capacitator* to the bulb. *Caution:* In some of the early outfits it was possible to get a shock from the equipment if carelessly handled because, while the voltage pressure from these units is small, the current is built up in excess of the current available from the dry cells themselves. The latest equipment guards against such shock.

The tiny batteries employed last about a year with ordinary use and they can be bought nearly all over the world. This is an advantage in traveling because dry cells of American make and size such as are used on old style flash equipment may not always be duplicated abroad.

Placing the flash equipment on a camera synchronized for its use is so easy that it takes only a few seconds to get set and be ready to shoot. This convenience and speed in operation are just new links in the chain of developments for making photography a cinch for everyone.

Indeed, so convenient and attractive has flash photography been made for the average person that the annual sale of flash lamps runs into hundreds of millions. It is almost no exaggeration to say that, without the use of flash lighting, many newspapers (particularly the picture tabloids) would find it impossible to function.

The greatest field for flash photography, apart from night-time use, lies in its ability to catch action. Thus, pictures taken by flash light reflect very realistically people's lives in movement, at the moment of greatest interest and drama. It is certainly not a technique for picturing people in static poses; that would be a waste of equipment.

The simplest method for taking flash pictures (one with which the beginner can scarcely miss) is with the flash bulb mounted on the camera. It is the method that is most commonly used and it does get results, providing exposures are applied with fair accuracy.

News photographers—who do not dare offer alibis for missed pictures—most generally use flash mounted in this manner. They haven't the time to experiment for pictorial values with press deadlines hanging over their heads like Damocles' sword. Even so, they manage to produce some very effective pictures with flash light directly on camera, and without any complicated maneuverings.

However, many photographers are beginning to tire of the stereotype results produced with this flat technique. Pictures with greater pictorial value and modeling can be produced with the flash bulb in other positions than directly at the camera.

One way to avoid the harsh, contrasty lighting peculiar to direct flash is to use flash as an indirect light on the subject. This can be done by aiming the flash gun at a ceiling or wall, while held in the hand away from the camera, in such a way as to bounce the light from the wall on the subject by the angle of reflection.

This method, apart from its superior pictorial effect due to the diffusion of the strong light, is especially favored in taking pictures of babies because it doesn't flash the strong light directly into their eyes. It should also be the method employed in taking pictures of persons known to be sensitive to strong light.

Results obtained in this manner are closer to the results obtained with natural light. Because the bounced light is less powerful than when it is used directly on the subject, it is necessary to compensate by increasing the exposure time. The lens should be opened at least one stop more than the exposure otherwise called for. And, if the surface from which the light is bounced is dark colored, an additional half stop could be used. Experience is the best guide in these matters.

As the photographer gains experience and more confidence, he can experiment with the flash bulb held to one side of the camera or higher or lower than the camera position. In addition, he can experiment with and perfect the method of using additional bulbs in extension units or in what are known as "slave" units, to broaden his effects and areas. Multiple-flash is the name used for this technique. As it is largely used by professionals on assignment for picture news magazine or other special work, it is outside the range of this discussion.

Battery flash is surely a great convenience in the matter of portability and freedom of movement, since batteries will furnish the necessary light wherever you are. But the bulbs are fairly expensive, the cost per shot ranging from 12¢-30¢. For anyone contemplating much flash work, there is available the more desirable electronic flash equipment. This equipment not only reduces the expense of flash work over a period but reduces also the bulk that transportation of a large number of bulbs presents.

In electronic flash, one permanent lamp is used and it is good for almost an indefinite number of flashes. The equipment may be bought for use on electric house current or with batteries (dry, or wet, nonspillable) or both. The weight ranges from about 3 pounds to well above 12 pounds, depending on the manufacturer, the bulb used, the kind of batteries employed, and the light ouput.*

If you take electronic flash equipment with you on your travels and if it employs house current, it may be necessary to include a matching transformer. Foreign current is not the same as ours, as many tourists have discovered to their dismay. Most commonly used in other parts of the world is 220 volts, 50 cycles. Even when current like ours is available, it is for 50 cycles; ours is 60 cycles. This doesn't do any harm and can be used for flash equipment, if not for a long period. Incidentally, 50-cycle current is useless for our electric clocks, which are made to run on 60 cycles.

Myself, I have never understood why anyone should want electronic flash equipped for house current "excitation," in *addition* to battery. Where house current is available, photofloods are not only cheaper, but more useful; #2 photofloods, mounted on the camera with a light-bar, will stop a fair amount of action. Electronic flash for *batteries,* however, seems like a miracle straight from heaven; it provides portability, quick action, convenience of movement. The photographer becomes completely independent of any other light source. The average unit of this kind wonderful though it is, costs about $60. That sum of money will buy close to 600 flash bulbs — now start calculating.

Flash photography can also be done with cameras not synchronized for flash work, Simply set the camera on "bulb" or "time" and use a hand-held flasher such as the Kodak Photo Flasher or the Victor Midget Flash Unit. Open the shutter, trigger the flash, close the shutter. The exposure afforded by this technique will be the duration of the light supplied by the bulb used. Since flash is only used under poor lighting conditions, the amount of exposure during the time shutter is open, but bulb hasn't yet flashed, is negligible.

Successful flash work involves the mastery of a few principles in exposure, which are easily learned. Manufacturers are constantly developing apparatus to make things easier for the photographer in this respect.

Elsewhere there will be found exposure tables to enable the photographer to get flash pictures with ease. Once you've taken some you will be astonished how simple the technique is and, before you know, you'll be experimenting with the best of them.

The smallest electronic flash on the market—and the only good photographic buy in France—is the French Rectaflex. It is made to slip easily into the accessory shoe of any camera and provides a very satisfactory light output.

TABLE I — FILM AND FLASH COMBINATION GUIDE NUMBERS

*LAMPS

FILM	Tungsten ASA		Bantam 8	PH-8	5-B	5	PR-25B	SM	SF	6	FP 26	**
Ektachrome B (Indoor)	16	Shutter speed		1/50 1/100 1/200	1/400	1/50 1/100 1/200	1/400	1/50 1/100 1/200	1/400	1/50 1/100 1/200	1/400	1/400
		Guide No.	110	95 70 55	55	95 80 65	50	60 50 42	36	95 65 40	36	36
Ansco Color (Indoor)	16	Shutter speed		1/50 1/100 1/200	1/400	1/50 1/100 1/200	1/400	1/50 1/100 1/200	1/400	1/50 1/100 1/200	1/400	1/400
		Guide No.	110	75 60	38	110 95	55	100 90 70	55	90 70 55	55	45
Kodachrome (Indoor)	12	Shutter speed		1/50 1/100 1/200	1/400	1/50 1/100 1/200	1/400	1/50 1/100 1/200	1/400	1/50 1/100 1/200	1/400	1/400
		Guide No.	60	44 34	28	80 65 50	45	50 48 45	38	80 45 35	35	25
Verichrome, Plenachrome, Plus-X Supreme	50	Shutter speed		1/50 1/100 1/200	1/400	1/50 1/100 1/200	1/400	1/50 1/100 1/200	1/400	1/50 1/100 1/200	1/400	1/400
		Guide No.	110	95 75	60	160 140 110	90	100 90 75	65	140 115 75	75	55
Tri-X and similar fast film	80	Shutter speed		1/50 1/100 1/200	1/400	1/50 1/100 1/200	1/400	1/50 1/100 1/200	1/400	1/50 1/100 1/200	1/400	1/400
		Guide No.	150	125 100	85	210 160 130	120	160 135 115	95	220 140 100	100	70

*Lamps listed are with bayonet base. These lamps can be duplicated (ask dealer) with screw-in base.

**Lamps in this column are for cameras with focal plane shutters.

For Ansco color film (indoor) use Filter UV-16
    " Ektachrome use Filter 81-EF
    " Kodachrome A use Filter 81-D

FLASH PHOTOGRAPHY

It would be advisable when using flash bulbs, especially at close distances to persons, to screen the bulb in some manner to avoid accidental shattering of the bulb. This is a rare occurrence but it's comfortable to know that there is some protection. A handkerchief will do. Photo shops also stock some devices to be used for this purpose. Usually, when using such a device, a small increase in exposure may be needed because of the light reduction.

How to Determine Your Flash Exposures by the Use of Flash Exposure Guide Numbers

After using Table 1 to get your flash guide number, the only other factor to determine is your lens opening. This can be done by dividing the guide number by the distance, in feet, of the lamp to subject. If the lamp is fixed on the camera, this means the distance of the camera from the subject. Some photographers like to use their lamps away from the camera position because they get better modeling that way. In that case, the lamp (not the camera) distance from subject is to be considered in the calculation.

TABLE 2

This table gives a handy range of f-stops for a few guide numbers, for quick reference (see preceding page).

Guide Number	Distance in feet Lamp to subject	F-Stop
65	6 feet	f/11
	9 "	f/8
	11 "	f/6.3
	16 "	f/4
	20 "	f/3.5 - 2.8
	30 "	f/2
75	6 "	f/16
	9 "	f/8
	11 "	f/6.3
	16 "	f/4.5
	20 "	f/3.5
	30 "	f/2.8
	40 "	f/2
100	6 "	f/16
	9 "	f/11
	11 "	f/8
	16 "	f/6.3
	20 "	f/4.5
	30 "	f/2.8

Exposures given are for 1/100 second, available on most cameras. That speed is chosen because it is not susceptible to camera shake. Data supplied by manufacturers. If good results are not obtainable, it is advisable to have your camera checked for accuracy of shutter operation. Shutters can be in error by as much as 100%.

For example, if your guide number is 65 and the lamp situated 10 feet from the subject, the lens opening should be 6.5 — the nearest lens stop is f/6.3, and there you are.

FILM AND FLASHBULB GUIDE

Here is a convenient guide to film and Flash used on simple cameras, equipped with flash-holder made by the same manufacturer. Some of these cameras can be equipped with other flash holders or adapters to take different base lamps than those shown.

GUIDE TO

Camera	Lamp No.	Film No.
Ansco Flash Clipper	5, 8	616
" Pioneer 16 } With JN-149 Flash	11	616
" Pioneer 20 } Unit Type I	5, 8	620
" Rediflex	5, 8	620
" Jr. Press	11	120
Argoflex 75	SM	620
Beacon II	11	127
Beacon 225	11	620
Bilora	5, 8, SM	120
Classic 35	5, 8	135
Clix Master Elite Flash	5, 8	127
Colonel Flash	5, 8	620
Comet Flash	11	
Compco Reflex	11	
Cruiser II	SM	
Cruiser 63	5, 8	
Dover	5, 8, SM	620
Empire	11	120
Falcon Flash	11	127
Faultless Flash	11	127
Fed-Flash	5, 8, SM	127
Foldex 20	5, 8	
Foldex Spectator	5, 8	
Foldex Traveler 120	11	120
Hopalong Cassidy Flash Camera	11	
Imperial	5, 8	620
Jom, Jr.	11	
Kodak Brownie Reflex	SM	127
" Brownie Flash 6-20	11	620
" Dua-Flex	SM	620
" Flash Brownie Hawkeye	5, 8	620
" Tourist with Kodet Lens	SM	620
Kodak Starmite Agi	M2	135
Pixie Flash	5, 8	*
Reflex 120	11	120
Reflex 620	11	620
Rival Flash 120	11	120
Rollex 20	5, 8	620 or 120
Rondine	SM	127
Roy Rogers Press Flash	5, 8	620
Spartaflex	11	120
Spartus 35-F	11	135
Spartus Full-vue	11	120
" Press Flash	11	120
" Reflex	11	120
" No. 4 Folding	11	120
Tower No. 34	11	120
Tower No. 51	5, 8	129 or 620
Tower No. 97	5, 8	120
Traveler 120	11	120
Trusite Minicam	11	127
Universal Univex Uniflash	11	*
" Meteor	5, 8	620
" Minute 16	5, 8	*
" Roamer	11	120 or 620
Vagabond 120	11	
Vu-Flash	5, 8	
Winpro 35 mm Flash	11	135
Winpro Synchro-Flash	SM	135
Wond-O-Flex	5, 8	620
Zenith Comet	5, 8	127

* Special film.

FLASH PHOTOGRAPHY

The World's Smallest Flashbulb

The least expensive and the safest flash bulb yet made was introduced recently by G.E., with imitators coming right along. The M-2 (as this latest bulb is called by G.E.) is only ¾" in diameter and has gained popularity rapidly because of its convenient size.

Two or more dozen can readily fit into one's coat pocket yet their efficiency (their light output) is such that very good black and white pictures can be taken at distances up to 15 feet with fast film and in box cameras. Good pictures can be obtained at even greater distances with cameras employing better lenses.

Yet the bulb is three cents cheaper than the price of regular size bulbs in use. It is necessary to employ an adapter to fit the bulb into the ordinary flash equipment but the adapter sells for pennies and is very simple to change over.

A bulb of this convenient type not only widens the use of flash bulbs but brings the technique within the means of the most humble photographic hobbyist, so far as expense goes.

ADVANTAGES IN THE USE OF FLASHBULBS

1 With Flashbulbs, you can take pictures *whenever* you want—in the early morning or evening, or at night—whenever you have a chance for a good picture.

2 With Flashbulbs, you can take pictures *wherever* you want—indoors at parties and dances, or outdoors on cloudy days or in the shade.

3 With Flashbulbs, you always know exactly how much light you have to take your picture. There's no guessing about exposures.

4 Because you don't have to guess at exposures, you take more good pictures per roll of film. Flashbulbs save you money on wasted film.

5 Flashbulbs fire so fast and are so sure that you can take action pictures even with inexpensive cameras with non-adjustable shutters.

6 Flashbulbs are easy to carry and use. You can always have plenty right at hand to capture those pictures you've always wanted.

—*Sylvania Electric Products, Inc.*

WHAT TO DO
ABOUT CLIMATIC CONDITIONS

(Some Precautions)

No special precautions are needed in *cool* climates, so far as the operation of your equipment or the preservation of your film is concerned. In very *cold* climates, however, difficulty may be experienced with the operation of the shutter in your camera; some shutters are fairly delicate.

This difficulty will manifest itself mainly in incorrect exposure due to the slowing down of shutter speeds. Never try to overcome this condition by oiling the shutter; it is not lubricated that way. Shutter repair or regulation is a job for an expert.

There's no way to estimate shutter mal-operation percentage-wise; it depends too much on the severity of the conditions with which you have to contend. Just keep adding to your normal exposure, little by little, till you hit upon the exposure that will do the trick under the conditions you face.

In the use of black and white film, shutter discrepancy, if not too great, will not ruin your shots; the liberal latitude in black and white film should, normally, take care of the matter. Color film, however, with its extremely small latitude, will be utterly ruined. If you are going to do much color work under unfavorable conditions, it would be best to make test shots and have them processed quickly. It's a procedure that may give you a sound basis for future exposure calculations.

It seems doubtful, though, that the average tourist will take himself to climates cold enough to make these difficulties an important factor. Trouble should not be experienced in any temperatures above zero.

A hot climate is another thing, especially one combined with high humidity. That can really play havoc with every part of your equipment. To guard against such climatic contingencies, it is essential that you keep your camera and film as cool as possible, and well aired. In addition, where the possibility of fungus mould exists, protect your camera and other pieces of equipment with adequate insulating cover —aluminum foil wrap, such as housewives use in the home, is excellent for the purpose.

When taking pictures on shipboard, on sandy beaches, or dusty roads, or any windy locations, clean your lens with soft tissue before picture-taking, Also try to protect your camera against the onslaught of waves, spray or sand. It's astonishing how fine sand can get into the tightest camera constructed. When sand does get into the camera, it can do considerable damage, the least of which might be the ruin of the film inside the camera at the moment.

So far as the actual technique of picture-taking under such conditions is concerned, be sure to hold the camera steady in the wind; camera shake is a common cause for failure and the loss of excellent shots, the opportunity for which may never occur again.

If your camera has a valuable lens, it would be well not to handle it too much for cleaning. It would be better if you did not have to clean it at all. Since, however, an occasional cleaning is a necessity, handle the camera with unusual care; if it is a snap-open camera, do not allow it to snap open violently but ease it out gently.

Good lenses are composed of several elements and violent action, under conditions of tropical heat, is liable to loosen and separate those elements; for all practical purposes that means a ruined camera.

Film Precautions

Special precautions are required with film too, and at every stage of the photographic process, from the loading of the camera, the actual picture-taking, the unloading, and, most important of all, the processing.

If you know in advance that you will encounter tropical conditions, you can purchase well-known makes of film with tropical wrapping; they are available in the larger photo shops.

Such film should not be unwrapped till just before using and, after exposures have been made, should be processed as soon as possible, lest the latent image deteriorate. In fact, never leave film in the camera for very long under tropical or sub-tropical conditions for the same reason.

Should you be unable to get the film processed promptly, store it away, *unsealed,* in its original container and in a cool place. If a household refrigerator is available which is operated at a moderate temperature and is not moist, that might do nicely as a storage place. However, even under such circumstances, it would be well not to store the film for more than a week.

After such storage, it will be necessary, before sending film away for processing, to dry it out by surrounding it with some moisture-absorbing material, of which there are many kinds suitable. The material most generally used is silica gel. If the local photo shop does not have it, the owner can tell you where to get it. Pharmacies should have it. An excellent new product, obtainable in hardware or housefurnishing stores in U.S., is "Absorb-Moist." For less than one dollar you can obtain enough to last for a lifetime of use for this particular purpose. And, it being of small bulk, you can take the material with you.

Climate Also Affects Picture-taking

Another feature of tropical countries for which allowances must be made is the actinic quality of the light. It is a condition which obtains, also, on or near mountain tops, at seashore, and in desert regions. The condition referred to is the intensity of the light.

Actually, the light is no more intense than in places with moderate climates; it only seems so. What happens is that light is radiated from more and brighter surfaces and from a sun that is more directly overhead. Deep shadows are cast into the areas in shade in contrast to the intense sunlight that prevails otherwise. The light contrast caused in this manner can be so great as to be outside the range that photographic emulsions can successfully render (reproduce).

If you have an exposure meter with you, it can give some guidance as to exposure for conditions of great contrast; some film instruction sheets do. The old-fashioned Burroughs Wellcome little handbook on exposures made mention of such conditions and gave data to meet them. This is a British publication, no longer issued, though it may yet be possible to get one in a large photo shop.*

In the final analysis, it may be impossible to take a picture satisfactorily under extreme light contrasts unless (1) you can use something as a light reflector to bounce light into the deep shadows—an ordinary white cardboard is just the thing; or (2) use what is known as a flash-bulb fill-in light. (See Flash section.)

Before arriving in any distant country, you may not know about the special climatic conditions prevailing there, except in general terms. Official information centers generally lack the technical background to judge the conditions as they affect photography. A reliable source of information will usually be found only on the spot. A very dependable source of such information is the local camera club, if one exists. Amateur camera clubs are abundant all over the world and one can generally be found. You can develop some wonderful contacts in this manner which can not only be helpful in specific situations but you can wind up with some permanent friedships. There's nothing like a mutual hobby for producing good will.

---

*The British Journal Photographic Almanac (an annual) contains an extensive analysis of exposures in all kinds of climates and lighting conditions. The tables are exhaustive and complicated but the person who is student enough to master the data supplied could dispense with an exposure meter for most outdoor conditions. Get it from Henry Greenwood Co., 24 Wellington St., Strand, London. Some American photo shops carry it, but the book sells out rapidly soon after it is issued.

BEWARE OF PHOTOGRAPHING THESE "ILLEGAL" SHOTS

The tourist need not be reminded that ours is an era of international tension and one in which a traveler is under the necessity to exercise a certain amount of discretion. Within the memory of many of the readers of this book, there was a time when a traveler could stalk the earth and could photograph anything within the range of his camera. Today, alas, such free-and-easy procedure could land one in the calaboose in foreign countries, even our own, as a suspicious character. Coming at a time when photography has become such a universal hobby, the situation is irksome indeed—but there it is.

It is quite unlikely that a tourist will want to photograph military installations or buildings anywhere. They are usually as ugly as the thing they represent; forbidding-looking, not photogenic at all. One can scarcely conceive of a tourist, knowingly, aiming his camera at them—in any case, it's forbidden.

However, the tourist might, unwittingly, get into trouble. Many such buildings have no openly military appearance and there may be nothing to identify them for what they are. The tourist may shoot them without any intention of violating regulations. Innocent or not, he may be called upon to do some tall explaining to win reprieve and to suffer no greater penalty than the confiscation of his film and, sometimes, even his camera.

In another section I've advised the tourist to inquire from local sources about the attractive subjects for photography available in the region in which he finds himself. When doing this, it is just as advisable to find out from these local sources what *not* to photograph.

The regulations of some foreign countries are briefly sketched here. The list is by no means complete. On the one hand regulations change frequently and on the other hand, many countries do not even wish to give the information. However, the list indicates a universal tendency and, to that extent, furnishes the tourist with an approximate idea of what his photographic behavior should be.

It might be noted, additionally, that while many countries prohibit photographing military personnel, it is not deemed objectionable to take pictures of soldiers when they take part in civic parades or fiestas. A reasonable assurance to this effect would be the presence of other photographers taking pictures on the scene, providing they look like amateurs and are not privileged newsmen.

What You Must Know When You Travel With A Camera

It is also advisable, when you enter a museum, to ask whether you may use your camera. In Europe, you may usually—but not always—photograph the interior of a church or cathedral; to be sure, ask. Castles or palaces, if privately owned, often impose restrictions. In Moslem countries, the farther west you go the stricter the restrictions about photographing people and religious interiors; ask at your hotel what are the local conditions.

BALI—This once famous paradise for photographers is, alas, no longer one. It is now strictly forbidden to photograph the half-naked photogenic gals of the country and it's healthy to obey the regulations. The country has recently acquired independence and is officious about its regulations.

BELGIUM—Official information bureau claims there are no restrictions of any kind. Play it safe with regard to military objects just the same.

DENMARK—There are no restrictions except the photographing of military grounds, the inside of museums (unless permission is granted), churches, and the Zoological Garden. Presumably the animals object or insist on model releases.

FINLAND—Military restrictions only. Special permits required at the Russian border.

FRANCE—Military areas forbidden, otherwise no restrictions. Cannot photograph inside of theatres. Most museums forbid carrying cameras inside; have to be checked on entry. In the Louvre, you pay an extra fee for carrying inside a handheld camera; you are then free to take snapshots. I was not allowed the use of a tripod, though.

GERMANY—As this is an occupied country, military installations are strictly under the regulations of the different occupying zonal authorities. They should be consulted if in doubt. Of course, there are no restrictions on the photographing of civilian subjects; as a matter of fact, photography is now, as it always has been, one of Germany's intense activities.

GREECE—A special permit, issued by the Ministry of Education, is required if the tourist wishes to photograph antiquities and museums. The permit is a slight formality and easily procured. You don't have to tip anyone to get quick action either. Other than that, no restrictions but use ordinary discretion. It was once forbidden to use tripods on the street but official informant advises that it can be done if interference with traffic is avoided.

GREAT BRITAIN—No restriction on the average run of picture-taking. Military installations to be avoided, of course. They are recognizable and Americans are extremely unlikely to get into difficulties. Permission may be necessary for picture-taking in certain exhibitions, the local authorities having jurisdiction in such cases. The "Beef-Eaters" on duty at London Tower are so accustomed to being photographed that every move they make is practically a studied pose. And everybody takes pictures of the changing of the guard at the Palace.

INDIA—One of the photogenic countries of the world. Happily, there are practically no restrictions. Watch out for religious taboos. In a land where there are hundreds of sects and religious sub-divisions, there are some customs that may cause trouble for the photographer. The obliging authorities will gladly advise about them. The natives of India are a gentle people and you may expect courteous treatment throughout the country.

ISRAEL—This little country has stringent regulations on photography. Cameras must be sealed 3 days before leaving the country. While Sabbath regulations are severe, cameras can be used but without flashlight. Certain areas are off-limits for cameras, the border regions, Jerusalem, etc.

JAPAN—Formerly (before the war), there were certain cities which were completely forbidden to photographers. This at a time when Japanese themselves were busily engaged in photographing the rest of the world. Now, the Japanese Travel Bureau advises, there are no restrictions.

MEXICO—(and Latin-American countries in general)—They're not so touchy about their military installations but are very sensitive about some other things. Never photograph the inside of a church. In the churches of Chichicastenango, Guatemala, this can make you the subject of violence. Do not shoot natives (Indians) unless they evidence amiability; they are superstitious about photography—it's best to ask permission. If permission is granted, you may be obliged to tip the model but that's better than having him tip you—into the lake.

NETHERLANDS—Apart from military objects, there are no restrictions and there is plenty of material for your camera. Windmills have to be searched for; they're not as common as may be supposed from looking at tourist literature.

NORWAY—No restrictions except military; particularly restricted are the northern areas of the country where most of these military installations exist.

PORTUGAL—The country's tourist authorities cannot give exact information about objects prohibited to photographers but they suggest that these are few and that regulations pertaining to them are similar to those in the U.S. In any case, no army installations or barracks or other government bodies should be photographed.

SPAIN—The tourist had better confine himself to conventional subjects: street scenes, people, fetes, bullfights, etc. If you are on a conducted tour to famous cathedrals and palaces, the guide will advise you if pictures may be taken inside such buildings. The palaces are generally fair game, and the famous remains of the Moorish occupation at Seville and Granada, Toledo, Cordova may be photographed freely.

SWEDEN—Only a few places in the northern parts of Sweden as well as in the Archipelago of Stockholm are considered protected areas to which foreigners need permits for transit travel. Naturally in these areas carrying cameras is prohibited. In addition, military installations anywhere are prohibited for photography. Having a few "spy" scares, Sweden is cautious. It is not difficult to identify forbidden areas, so no trouble should be expected. The Swedes are a civilized people and photographing them in their daily activities is one of the pleasantest aspects of travel there.

SWITZERLAND—The country prohibits photographing military installations or buildings and suggests that you watch out for signposts which identify such prohibited areas.

SOUTH AFRICA—No restrictions. However, the country is in a political turmoil and discretion might well be exercised. Avoid, whenever possible, an area of civil disturbance.

YUGOSLAVIA—This country, magnificent to photograph, is one in which the tourist has to be careful. I know from experience that it is not permitted to photograph trains, railway stations, coastal areas, government buildings, and any kind of civil disturbance. If the photographer confines himself (as in Spain) to conventional subjects and innocuous scenery, he should have no trouble. If you can identify yourself as an innocent tourist, the worst that can happen in doubtful situations is confiscation of your film. Your camera may be returned, if you're lucky. Film very expensive, processing poor.

In some places it's illegal to take any pictures at all. Flying over the Panama Canal, your camera will be taken from you during the flight. Another detail: Taking pictures inside of churches in Latin-America can lead to difficulties, yet, in Europe it's done all the time. In fact, American Catholics are frequently outraged by the irreverence with which, apparently, Europeans treat their churches. In Italy, children play in them; informal gatherings for gossip and mutual visits take place there; in short, the people practically live in the churches. They certainly do not object to taking pictures in or around them.

To sum the matter up, a camera can be a lot of fun, but it's no fun to get into difficulties because of it and there's no necessity to do so. If in doubt, consult the nearby gendarme, the local travel office, or an American Consulate. Incidentally, I've never understood why American travelers make so little use of our consulates abroad. They are in existence to serve Americans and are glad to do so. They are thoroughly familiar with local conditions and are staffed with local people. It is an excellent idea, when traveling in the more backward countries off the beaten path, to register with the nearest American Consulate and to notify the Consulate when you leave the country. The procedure may never be important, but when it is, it's vital. (The Consul may also be able to get you out of small difficulties with local authorities but don't crowd your luck.)

PROCESSING YOUR FILM WHEN YOU TRAVEL

To get good processing in foreign countries represents one of the greatest difficulties in travel. Norman Ford, the well-known travel writer, reports that many of his films mailed to processers in big European cities were lost in transit. Some of them took months to trace; others were never found. Those that were found not only lost their timeliness but the delay caused their latent image to deteriorate past redemption. However, Ford had no alternative; he did not dare get processing done in the primitive places from which he mailed the film. His poor luck in this case was one of the fortunes of travel, like war.

Processing for commercial reproduction cannot be left to the mercies of the average photo shop, in which processing is really only a sideline. This is true not only in the U.S., where most of the work is done in mechanized factories calling themselves "labs," and offering no individual attention, but it is even true abroad, where automatic mechanism is not generally employed and the work is subject *solely* to individual attention.

Individual attention is fine in theory but it can be a mixed blessing in foreign countries. I have often felt that I would rather trust myself to automatic processing than to the vagaries of incompetent handcraftsmen.

Sometimes, as a result of this hand-work, you may get astonishingly fine quality at prices considerably below those prevailing in the U.S. Sometimes you may get work inferior even to the local "drugstore" processing at home. Elsewhere in the book there appears a list of some establishments in foreign countries which personal experience (my own and others') has found to be dependable and, in some cases, superb.

An interesting fact which may not be known to many is the possibility of having your black and white film processed on your passenger ship while crossing the ocean. Not only do the large passenger liners carry a ship's photographer, but his laboratory is available for processing the passengers' film and for making prints and enlargements.

The prices charged by these ship's photographers are, in most cases, less than those at home and the work is usually excellent. Of necessity, the work is done quickly—you need not fear it will not be completed before ship's landing; the photographer will not take it on if he can't deliver on time for the landing. No tipping is necessary since the work is fully paid for when delivered.

Processing Your Film When You Travel

The ship's photographer is often called upon for various small services of a photographic nature. He will load film for you in his dark room, if your equipment is of a nature requiring such procedure. Also, likely as not, he is competent to make small repairs and many a jammed camera or film has been put back into condition by an obliging ship's photographer.

If he's a pleasant guy (and I've never encountered any other), you can strike up an acquaintance with him; he will probably allow you to see the operation of his compact but practical little laboratory.

If you are traveling on a freighter, a form of travel that is becoming increasingly popular, the ship's officer would undoubtedly be willing to find some quarter that you could rig up as a dark room to do your own processing, if you have the equipment and are competent to do it. Freighter officers, in these and other matters, are obliging beyond anything you could expect on regular passenger liners.

Should you be able to set up a dark room, you will probably have a lot of work thrust on you by some of the other passengers. At a price, of course. Naturally, there's no money in it for you, really, but it would be a godsend as a method for whiling away the time on a long freighter voyage, if you are a restless person. Also, it would set you up as a special person to whom all gratitude would be due.

When mailing film for processing, either to the U.S. or to the Eastman and Ansco agencies abroad, more care must be exercised than with your regular mail. If the film has been dried (see the instructions elsewhere for using your camera in the tropics), it can be mailed in the special mailing tubes supplied by the film manufacturers or obtainable in photo shops.

A gummed label can be glued around the tube; it acts as a seal and at the same time provides a place where you can carefully *print* the address. Be sure to *print* a return address too and allow sufficient time for processing so that the return address you supply will be the one which will locate you when the processed work is mailed back. Be liberal in your calculations—foreigners do not believe in rushing themselves.

The most difficult thing is the postage. It is almost certain to be an amount which cannot be obtained in one stamp but which will require several stamps. It takes ingenuity to find room for several stamps on a mailing tube as small as the one furnished for 35mm and other popular size rolls of color film.

Sometimes, you may find it necessary to send a larger package (with the tube inside) just to make room for the stamps required. Then, ironically, (it has happened to me often), there may exist a single stamp of the denomination required for the larger package. That's what makes life interesting for the traveler.

If you value the film, register it. The extra expense is not great and it has often saved film for many photographers—though it may follow them around a continent before it catches up with them.

The package should also contain some description of its contents on the outside. The precise wording to be used may be found in the section dealing with Customs Regulations elsewhere. If the film being sent is fast panchromatic film, you had better add a caution to the effect that if the package is to be opened for inspection it should be done in complete darkness lest the film be spoiled. There is a division of opinion regarding the necessity to do this but I have always done so and have never lost a roll as a result.

The gummed labels supplied by the manufacturers of color roll film to be used for mailing purposes have printed on them the information that satisfies most postoffice inspectors. But this information applies to color film only and might be inadequate for black and white film.

In sending film to the U.S. for processing, registered air mail is preferred to air express; it is generally cheaper and the time factor as between the two methods is negligible. I have sent film by ordinary surface mail without loss or damage.

Mark your package as follows:

"Exposed amateur film being sent for processing. Amateur pictures exclusively—for no commercial purpose whatsoever."

If the package is too small to contain the message, it can be written on a shipping tag attached to the package.

Some Additional Processing Hints

You may find it necessary to have photo enlargements made while abroad instead of waiting till you return and thus be compelled to entrust the work to a local photo shop. If the work proves unsatisfactory, the local photographer should be willing to do the work over again but he may not have full knowledge of the cause of the defects of which you complain or what to do about them.

The DuPont Mfg. Co. issues a very helpful guide in this matter and with it you could point out to the local processor what needs to be done to remedy matters. Moreover, the guide is one that may also be of future value to you. Here it is:

Cause and Prevention of Print Defects

The majority of common print defects are caused by use of exhausted solutions, careless handling or neglect in following instructions for the proper use of materials.

Defect	Cause	How to Prevent
Yellow stain	Exhausted fixing bath Forced development	Keep hypo fresh Use recommended developing time Keep developer fresh
	Weak or exhausted developer Insufficient washing	Provide constant agitation, and flow of water

Defect	Cause	How to Prevent
Fog	Safelight too strong	Check safelight; follow manufacturer's recommendations
	Light-struck paper	Keep paper in light-proof packages
	Overdevelopment	Give proper exposure
	Improperly compounded developer	Follow formulas accurately
Abrasion	Rubbing of paper	Handle paper carefully
Blisters	Warm fixers or stop-baths	Keep solutions as near 68°F (20°C) as possible
Gray or granular appearance	Paper stored in damp atmosphere	Keep paper in cool, dry place
	Forced development & underexposure	Develop for recommended time and exposure
Flatness	Dirty enlarger lens	Clean darkroom equipment
	Trace of fog	Use proper safelight; avoid excessive exposure
Fingerprints	Improper handling	Insure cleanliness; use print tongs;
Fine spots	Chemical dust in room	Don't mix chemicals in darkroom
	Undissolved chemicals in solution	Mix thoroughly and carefully
	Dust or dirt	Keep darkroom clean
Veiled spots	Lack of agitation and separation in developers and fixing baths	If more than one print is prepared at a time, agitate and separate each sheet
	Old fixing baths	Keep solution fresh

If You Can Do Your Own Processing*

There's a new developing tank** on the market so easy to use that the veriest tyro can now undertake to do his own film developing, whether at home or when traveling. In that way the tourist can be assured of the kind of processing he wants plus the added advantage that he will not have to store exposed film for lack of suitable processing shops. Storing exposed film, as previously explained, is always a hazard because it results in loss of film speed and in deterioration of the image.

The tank is self-loading, self-threading, takes only seconds to load. The loading is smooth and the film cannot scratch or buckle in the process. All sizes, from 35mm to #116, whether black and white or color, can be successfully handled.

It is a simple matter, with a developing tank of this kind, to carry prepared chemical developers in small units such as are stocked in photo shops everywhere and, presto: you are independent of all film processing difficulties.

Once the film has been developed, it can be stored safely for an indefinite period without risk of deterioration; when you get back home you can make prints and enlargements to meet your requirements.

There are some details so often neglected that a large photo-finishing firm has gone to the trouble of issuing a list of the common causes for

---
*There are now more than a million amateur photographers who do their own processing; the number is growing daily as the amateur discovers how easy, economical and convenient home processing is to do.
**Ansco Developing Tank. It can be bought separately or included in the Ansco 3A Home Developing Outfit. This is a complete compact unit containing all the materials necessary except film chemical developers.

failure. On the basis of years of experience with work for amateurs, they find the following defects are the most common.

Common Faults in NEGATIVES

Not sharp or blurred	—Caused by object moving too fast —Out of focus —Camera shake during exposure; use tripod
Too Light	—Lens opening too small —Light too weak —Too short exposure; more time needed
Blank Prints	—Failure to set shutter —Failure to press button —Failure to take off lens cap
Double Exposure	—Something in front of lens—perhaps a finger —Failure to turn film between exposures. Make it a rule to advance film after every shot
Dark Smears	—Caused by light entering the camera —Light struck while loading or unloading; camera should always be loaded in deep shade, especially when using fast film
Too Dark	—Taking pictures against strong light or sun —Overexposure—use small lens stop

These Faults Can Be Corrected

The correction of most of these faults comes with experience, of course, and is under your control to the extent that you gain that necessary experience. Photography, at least as practiced by the amateur, is not a difficult technique and the defects noted can be overcome with just a little added care. The results will be rewarding in the increased satisfaction you will gain from your work.

Making Prints for Commercial Purposes

In the making of prints for commercial purposes, extreme enlargements are not necessary. Many amateurs, when trying their hands at selling their photos for the first time, think huge enlargements will clinch the sale; actually, they tend to disclose minor defects which, otherwise, might not be noticeable. While 8″ x 10″ prints are most often used commercially because most pictures files are made for that size, 5″ x 7″ is adequate if the subject is interesting enough to be acceptable.

The print must be made on glossy paper and polished to a high finish by ferrotype. A ferrotype is a metal plate on which glossy prints are dried and afterwards peeled off. The process imparts a mirror-like glaze. Such a finish is an absolute requirement for fine detail reproduction in smooth-paper magazines. It is even more necessary for newspaper reproduction because a considerable amount of detail is lost in the coarse screen plates employed on newspapers.

Photo Dealers and Processing Establishments

The names below are those of photo dealers and processing establishments whose reliability has been established either by the author's personal experience or the experience of tourists known to the author. Unless, unlike the leopard, any of them has changed his spots, you may expect honorable treatment and processing of good quality, at their hands.

ADEN. S. E. Delbourgo (Aden) Ltd., Steamer Point, Aden.
A. Besse Co., Steamer Point
ARGENTINE. Rossi & Lavarello, S.R.L., Corrientes 678, Buenos Aires.
Gevaert Argentina S.A. de Productos Fotograficos, Bartolome Mitre 1902, Buenos Aires.
Kodak Argentina, Alsina 951, Buenos Aires
AUSTRALIA. H. Bleakley Photographics Pty. Ltd., 397/399 Kent Street, Sydney.
R. Gunz Pty., 11-c Castlereagh St., Melbourne.
Kodak Pty. 37 Rundle St., Adelaide
Kodak Pty. 259 Queen St., Queensland
Herbert Small, 243 Pitt St., Sydney.
AUSTRIA. Wachtl, Graben 21, Vienna.
Johann Kraus, Jacquingasse 29, Vienna
C. Knodler Co., Theobaldgasse 15, Vienna.
C. Knodler & Co., Webgasse 2a, Vienna VI.
Photo City, Kaerntnerstrasse 45, Vienna.
Photo Rosner, Schottengasse 4, Vienna.
Photo Rottmayer, An der Staatsbruecke, Salzburg.
Herlango, Marie Theresienstrasse 10, Innsbruck.
Photo Seka, Burggraben, Innsbruck.
Photo Herlango, Herrengasse, Graz.
Photo Herlango, Landstrasse, Linz.
BELGIUM. Photo-Monde, 13 rue les Sables, Brussels.
J. Haesaerts & Fils, Marche St. Jasques 9, Antwerp
Socophar, Rue de la Science 5, Brussels.
Kodak S.A. 21, Ave. de la Toison d'Or Brussels.
BERMUDA. Bermuda Cigar Store, Hamilton
The Camera Store, Queen St., Hamilton
Yankee Store, Queen St., Hamilton
BRAZIL. Brasport, Ltda., Rua Aurora 955 Sao Paulo; also at Rua Mexico 128-2° Slj. Rio de Janeiro.
Foto Productos Gevaert do Brasil S.A, Rua Mayrink Veiga 31-C, Rio de Janeiro.
Kodak Brasileira, Campo de Sao Cristovao 268, Rio de Janeiro.
BRITISH GUIANA. Acme Photographic Supplies, 124 Regent and King Streets, Georgetown.
BOLIVIA. Casa Kalvin, Potosf 259, La Paz.
BURMA. D. A. Ahuja, 128 Sale Pagoda Rd., Rangoon.
CANADA. Arrow Films Ltd., 213 Adelaide Street West, Toronto.
CEYLON. Chas. Gouldson Ltd., Imperial Bank Buildings, Colombo.
Millers Co. 702 Galle Road, Colombo.
CHILE. Mario Vargas Rosas, Casilla 4219 — Miraflores 562, Santiago de Chile.
Kodak Chilena, Alonso Ovalle 1188, Santiago
COLOMBIA. Casa Belga, Verswijvel & Co., Apartado Aereo 3087, Calle 13.
Nos. 15-69/15-73, Bogota.
Kodak Colombiana, Carrera 13, Bogota
COSTA RICA. Sancho Ardon, San Jose.
Federspiel & Co., San Jose.
CYPRUS. Sheridan (Orient) Ltd., 53/55 Tricoupi Street, Nicosia.

CUBA. Kodak Cubana, 23, No. 156 Vedado, Havana.
DENMARK. Kongsbak & Cohn, Vimmelskaftet 43, Copenhagen.
J. Polack, Vestergade 12a, Copenhagen.
Thorbild Henriksen Skoubogade 4, Copenhagen.
Kodak Aktieselskab, Ostersadel, Copenhagen
E. Wessel, Ryesgade 19-21, A., Copenhagen — N.
SANTO DOMINGO. J. D. Guerrero, 28 El Conde, Ciudad Trujillo.
ECUADOR. Casa Lopez, Guayaquil 827, Quito.
EGYPT. W. A. Lancaster & Son, 11 Emad El Dine Street, Cairo, and at Alexandria.
Kodak S.A., 2, Rue Istamboul, Alexandria.
EIRE. Slattery Allan & Co. Ltd, 162 Parnell Street, Dublin.
EL SALVADOR. Sanchez & Co. Delgado 18, San Salvador
FRANCE. Foto Shop, Place Massena, Nice, Riviera.
Harry's, 21 Champs-Elysee, Paris.
Exclusivites Telos, 35 Rue de Clichy, Paris.
Kodak-Pathe, 28 Place Vendome, Paris.
FINLAND. Valokuvaustarpeisto Helios, Mannerheimintie 10, Helsinki.
Valokuvaustarpeisto Helios, Keskustori 5, Tampere.
Oy. Foto Ab., Eerikinkatu 17, Turku.
Oy. Foto Ab., Rauhankatu 16, Lahti.
Nyblins-Magasin A.B., Mannerheimvagen, 20, Helsinki.
GERMANY. Porst Photo Co., Nuremberg.
Voigtlander A. G., Campestrasse 7, Braunschweig.
Fotohaus Kleinholz, Hohestrasse 112, Koeln.
Gustav Henry Helms, Kuhmuhle 10, Hamburg.
Foto-Kundt, Mommsenstrasse 64, Berlin-Charlottenburg.*
Foto-Schaja, Maximilianstrasse 32, Muenchen.
Thimmer & Wittenberg, Luisenstrasse, Hannover.
Fotohaus Leistenschneider, Schadowstrasse 19, Duesseldorf.
Foto-Binder, Koenigtrasse 38, Stuttgart.
Weizsaecker, 2 Quebingerstr. 1, Stuttgart.
Fotohaus Leppin, Motzstrasse 68, Berlin W 30.
Photo-Rahn, Kaiserstrasse 76, Frankfurt a.M.
GIBRALTAR. A. G. Day & Sons, 14 Bomb House Lane, Gibraltar.
GOLD COAST. N.V. H.v. J. F. Sick & Co., Kumasi and Accra.
GREAT BRITAIN. Wallace Heaton, 28 Old Bond St., London.
Dollonds, 281 Oxford St., London.
Warnes, 5 Marsh St., Bristol.
John Saville Sons, 4 Goodramate, York.
Sheffield Photo, 6 Norfolk Row, Sheffield.
John Campbell Harper, 131 Leith Walk, Edinburgh.
Processing: Autotype Co. Brownlow Rd., West Ealing, London.

* Russian zone

R. Fox Hampstead, High St., London
City Engraving Co., Ryde Ave., Hull (Yorks)
Norward Inglis, 22 Ainslie Place, Edinburgh.
GREECE. F. Ranios, 14 Churchill St., Athens.
S. D. Skouras, 5 Santarosa St. Athens.
T. J. Spyrides, Rue Char Trikoupi, Athens.
GUATEMALA. Foto Alvarez, 6 Ave. Sur 21, Guatemala City.
Isabel de Legrand, 6a Avenida 9-37, Guatamala.
HAITI. Mohr Sales Co. 48 Rue Roux, Port-au-Prince.
HAWAII. Kodak Hawaii, 1065 Kapiolani Blvd. Honolulu.
HOLLAND. E. Fischel, Jr. N.V. Gelderschekade 88, Amsterdam, C.
HONG KONG. H. M. Hodges Ltd., 1/47/8 Alexandria House.
Kodak Ltd. Edinburgh House, Hong Kong.
INDIA. Allied Photographics Ltd., Kasturi Building, Jamshedji Tata Road, Bombay, 1, and Branches at Calcutta, Madras and New Delhi.
Photographic Stores and Agency, 154 Darmtalla St., Calcutta.
R. N. Ahuja, 201 Hornby Rd., Fort, Bombay.
Bombay Photo Stores, 33 Park Mansion, Calcutta.
Kodak Limited, 2/155 Mount Road, Madras.
INDONESIA. N. V. Handels v.h., Reiss & Co., Djakarta.
IRAQ. A. R. Thaddeus, 406 B/1 Rashid Street, Baghdad.
IRELAND. Kodak Limited, 89 Grafton St. Dublin.
ISRAEL. A. Berner, 15 Rothschild Blvd., Tel-Aviv.
Fotofilm, 84 Allenby Road, Tel-Aviv.
Photo Prisma, Zion Square, Jerusalem.
Photo Eden, 3 Ben Yehuda St., Jerusalem.
Photo Brenner, 31 Hehalutz St., Haifa.
ITALY. La Meccanaptica, Corso Italia 8, Milan.
Kodak, Via Nazionale, 26, Rome.
Kodak, Via Vittor Pisani 16, Milan.
JAMAICA. Lamberts Camera Corner, 72 East Queen Street, Kingston.
Stanley Motta, 109 Harbour St. Kingston.
JORDAN (HASHEMITE KINGDOM OF THE). Hagop Berberian & Son, P.O. Box 209, Amman.
KENYA. A. H. Wardle & Co., Ltd., Post Box 193, Nairobi.
LEBANON &
SYRIA. Gabriel S. Antaki, B.P. 1236, Beyrouth.
MALAYA. Diethelm & Co. Ltd., 139/149b Market Street, Singapore.
Lee & Sons, 189 High St., Kuala Lumpur.
MALTA. Cutajar & Co. 12 Paul St., Valletta.
Day, Son & Miller, 32 b South Street, Valetta.
MEXICO. Sanborn's, Monterrey.
Julio, S.A. Colon 125, Guadalajara.
American Photo, Madero 21, Mexico City.
Foto Products, Ave. Hidalgo, Oaxaca.
Kodak Mexicana, Londres16, Mexico City.
NETHERLANDS (insert under Holland)
Anna Paulownastraat 76, The Hague
NEW ZEALAND. H. E. Perry, Auckland.
Kodak Ltd. 18 Victoria St., Wellington.
NIGERIA. United Africa Co. Ltd., Photographic Dept., P.O. Box 559, Lagos.
NORWAY. Gerth. Ludvigsen, A/S, Dronningensgt, 34, Oslo.

Magnus Boysen & Co., A.S., H. Heyerdahlsgt. 1 (for Photographic products), Oslo.
J. Nerlien, Nedre Slottsgate 13, Oslo.
PAKISTAN. Allied Photographics (Pakistan) Ltd., Habib Bank Building, Victoria Road, Karachi, 3.
Allied Photographics (Pakistan) Ltd., Qamar House (First Floor), Bunder Road, Karachi.
PANAMA. Kodak Panama, 98 Ave. Central, Panama.
PERSIA. M. Babajanian, Avenue Shah, Teheran.
PERU. Kodak Peruana, Pacae 946, Lima.
PHILIPPINES. Kodak Philippines, 104 13th St., Manila.
PORTUGAL. Garces Limitada, Rua Garrett 88, Lisbon.
J. C. Alvarez, 205 Rua Augusta, Lisbon.
Focar Limitada, Rua da Fabrica, Oporto.
Paris em Coimbra, Rua da Sofia 52, Coimbra.
Agencia Comercial do Mondego, Av. Sa Bandera 2, Coimbra.
Kodak Portuguesa, Rua Garrett 33, Lisbon.
PORTUGUESE E. AFRICA. R. Lobo Lda., P.O. Box 526, Lourenco Marques.
PUERTO RICO. Matias Photo, 200 Fortaleza St., San Juan.
Gonzalez & Co., Plaza Corner Christina St. Ponce
RHODESIA (S & N.). Peterhouse, Ltd., 17 Manica Road, Salisbury.
SIAM. Diethelm & Co. Ltd., Bangkok.
SOUTH AFRICA. Peterhouse, Ltd., 3-22 Barrack Street, Cape Town.
Kodak Pty. 339 West St., Durban
Kodak Pty. Rissik St. Johannesburg
SPAIN. Importadora Cinematografica Fotografica, Paseo de la Castellana 13, Madrid.
Industria Fotoquimica Nacional S.A. 48, Calle Buenos Aires, Barcelona.
Kodak S.A., Paseo de Gracia 22, Barcelona
Kodak S.A., Av. de Jose Antonia 6, Madrid.
SWEDEN. Hugo Svensson & Co., Fotoakt, Storgaten 13, Goteborg.
Fotoagenturen A.B.—Master Samuelsgatan 23, Stockholm.
Hasselblads Fotografiska A.B., Hamngatan 16, Stockholm.
Hasselblads Fotografiska A.B., Hamngatan 41-43, Goteborg.
SWITZERLAND. Perrot, S.A., Bienne.
Foto Bachmann, Burklihof, Clariden-Str. Zurich.
Hausamann Co., Bahnhof Str. 91, Zurich.
Hausamann Co., Marktgasse 13, St. Gallen.
Foto Jeck, Gerbergasse 80, Basel.
Photohaus Bischhausen, Marktgasse 53, Bern.
Photohaus Amrein-Graf, 27 Quai des Bergues, Geneva.
Kodak S.A. 13, Av. Jean-Jacques Mercier, Lausanne.
SYRIA. Kodak, Fardoss St., Damascus.
TANGANYIKA. A. H. Wardle & Co. Ltd., Post Box 224, Dar Es Salaam.
TANGIER. Casa Ros, Blvd. Pasteur, 8/14.
TRINIDAD. Harriman & Co., 61 Marine Sq. Port-of-Spain.
TURKEY. Lumiyer, Istiklal Caddesi 519/21, Tunel Meydani, Istanbul.
Kodak, 3 Ensiz Sokak, Istanbul.
UGANDA. A. H. Wardle & Co. Ltd., Post Box 103, Nairobi.
URUGUAY. Kodak, Colonia 1222, Montivideo.
VENEZUELA. Micron C. A., Edificio Karam, Ibarras a Pelota, Apartado 2445, Caracas.
VIRGIN ISLANDS. Axel Ovesen, St. Croix.

Processing Your Film When You Travel   75

COLOR PROCESSING OUTSIDE THE UNITED STATES

The following establishments are equipped to process all Eastman color film, black and white film, still and cine film in 8 and 16 mm

ARGENTINA. Kodak Argentina Calle Alsina 951, Buenos Aires.*

AUSTRALIA. Kodak Pty., Abbotsford, N. 9, Melbourne.

BELGIUM. Kodak S.A. 43 Rue de Stassart, Brussels.*

BRAZIL. Kodak Brasileira, Caixa Postal 849, Rio de Janeiro.*

CANADA. Canadian Kodak, Toronto 9, Ontario.

CHILE. Kodak Chilena, Casilla 2797, Santiago.*

COLOMBIA. Kodak Colombiana, **Apartado** Nacional 810, Bogota.*

CUBA. Kodak Cubana, Apartado 1349, Havana.*

DENMARK. Kodak Aktieselskab, Vodroffsvej 26, Copenhagen.*

EAST AFRICA. Kodak, Ltd. Box 28, Nairobi, Kenya.*

EGYPT. Kodak S.A. Box 527, Cairo.*

EIRE. Kodak Ltd. Rathmines, Dublin.*

ENGLAND. Kodak, Ltd. Box 14, Wealdstone, Harrow, Middlesex.

FRANCE. Kodak-Pathe S.A. Ave. Victor Hugo, Sevran.

GERMANY. Kodak A.G., Hedelfingerstrasse 56, Stuttgart.**

HAWAII. Kodak Hawaii, Box 1260, Honolulu.

HOLLAND. Kodak N.V. Anna Paulownastraat 76, the Hague.*

INDIA. Kodak Ltd. Box 343, Bombay 1.

ITALY. Kodak, Via Vittor Pisani 16, Milan*

MEXICO. Kodak Mexicana, **Londres 16,** Mexico City.

NORWAY. J. Nerlien A/S, Nedre Slottsgate 13, Oslo.*

PANAMA. Kodak Panama, Apartado 789, Panama.*

PERU. Kodak Peruana, Casilla 2557, Lima.*

PHILIPPINES. Kodak Philippines, 104 13th St., Manila.***

PORTUGAL. Kodak Portuguesa, Rua **Garrett** 33, Lisbon.*

SINGAPORE. Kodak Ltd., Box 687, Singapore.*

SOUTH AFRICA. Kodak Pty. 102 Davies St. Johannesburg.

SPAIN. Kodak S.A. Irun 15, Madrid.*

SWEDEN. Hasselblads Foto AB, Spanga.

SWITZERLAND. Kodak S.A. 13, Ave. Jean-Jacques Mercier, Lausanne.***

URUGUAY. Kodak Uruguaya, Colonia 1222, Montevideo.*

* Black and white cine film only.
** All color film but not black and white cine film.
*** All film but not color cine film.

WHAT EQUIPMENT SHOULD YOU TAKE?

The kind of equipment that is useful and suitable for a traveler will be somewhat different from what he would consider necessary in his own home territory.

Obviously, there must be considerd the limitations imposed by convenience, weight and bulk. For example, very few travelers, it may be assumed, would care to be burdened with processing equipment abroad, no matter how enthusiastic in their hobby they may be or the difficulties of obtaining suitable processing where they are traveling. This, despite the fact that equipment available today is a far cry from the days when traveling photographers, like the famous American, Brady, were forced to transport their equipment on heavily-laden pack mules because of the huge bulk and weight.

The following equipment, listed in the order of importance, comprises the most the average tourist would consider possible to take with him:*

Camera
Film
Filters and accessories
Tripod
Simple developing tank and chemicals

The Camera

The choice of a camera is completely dependent on what you want out of it. Notwithstanding beguiling advertising, there is no one ideal camera for all purposes. While all cameras are basically alike (except for one, which will be described later), their operations vary over a wide range. Basically, they all consist of a light-tight box or enclosure, with provision for holding a film rigidly in place, a lens for transmitting light to the film, a shutter to measure off the time of exposure, and a provision for focusing or viewing the subject of the photograph.

There are multitudinous differences in the methods whereby these functions are performed, the convenience of operation, the flexibility with which the instrument can be manipulated to further the photographer's purpose, the accuracy and speed with which that purpose can be accomplished, and the size of the negative (picture) to be obtained.

---

*I doubt that anyone would take along an enlarger, though a professional might do so. If you plan to take an enlarger, you might investigate the most compact one available today: the Federal Store-Away Model 240. In its carrying carton, it measures 15"x13"x9" and will accommodate negatives up to 2¼"x3¼".

Naturally, the more refinements in workmanship and mechanism imparted to an instrument, the more expensive it becomes. Therefore, each individual will have to weigh for himself the cost of the instrument against what he hopes to accomplish in photography.

The Box Camera

The simplest camera of all is the ubiquitous box camera — it is well-nigh universal. Of it, it might be accurate to say that you press the button and all the rest will be done for you. It has the utmost simplicity of operation; so simple, indeed, that children do very satisfactory work with it and adult photographers would do well not to sneer at its performance either.

It has practically a universal fixed focus; that is, the object to be photographed is in sharp focus from about 6 feet to infinity. Infinity, photographically speaking, means out to the end of what is visible. The camera is easily loaded and unloaded and comes in a range of sizes accommodating most of the popular and inexpensive roll films.

There is no more practical way to make a start in photography than with the use of a box camera because it is so inexpensive to operate. And the results, within the limitations of the camera, are excellent for average purposes; indeed, some professional photographers, as a stunt, have taken very good pictures with a box camera to demonstrate that it can be done. Anyhow, one can have a lot of fun with a box camera.

But it has definite limitations, the most serious one being its lack of flexibility. The box camera is useless in poor light, even with fast film. If it is possible to use a time exposure (most box cameras have that provision), that's what has to be done, outdoors, in deep shade. In short, it is only capable of taking satisfactory pictures in bright shade or in direct sunlight. Then, too, its slow, fixed shutter speed does not allow the stopping of the slightest action. And, in addition, the simple lens employed does not yield a negative with a quality that would permit the making of acceptable enlargements.

Many box cameras, today, are equipped with flash-light equipment. This overcomes one of the limitations of the camera for it extends its picture-taking possibilities to interiors, to night-time shots, and even to shots by poor daylight; in the last-named situation, the flash can be used as a fill-in light. Nevertheless, the box camera, simple and excellent though it may be, still remains a limited instrument, incapable of the precision results desired by the advanced photographer.

The Miniature Camera

There is an important range of cameras, which are generically called "miniature" cameras because of their small size and the tiny negatives obtained. While cameras using 35mm film are generally the cameras designated in this manner, actually there should be included the fairly large number of cameras yielding negatives smaller than 35mm. These cameras yield still picture negatives as small as 8 mm.

The true, the original miniature camera: the 35mm camera, is a small, compact, light-weight, and easily-transported camera. It comes in several types just like its larger brothers: folding, collapsible, and reflex.

Most of the better ones are equipped with coupled rangefinders whereby sharp focusing is automatically accomplished just by racking out the lens, to which the rangefinder is coupled. Miniature cameras may also be had with reflex focusing and there are several imported models which have a combination of both types of focusing on the one camera. Each type has its devotees and each does excellent work.

The miniature type of camera first came into prominence when it was employed by its inventor to take unobtrusive tiny pictures of various famous personages in Europe, while they were relaxed and unaware that their pictures were being taken. His achievements along this line were sensational.

As a result, the miniature camera has been called the "candid" camera. The nomenclature is not accurate because "candid" applies to a method rather than to an instrument. However, it is undoubtedly true that the method was ushered in by the 35mm camera and the camera is well suited to it.

In the hands of skillful workers, to whom precise and fastidious processing is a carefully acquired discipline, the miniature has produced superb results. Because of the small negative size, processing is the critical point in miniature photographic techniques. The film must be developed with fine-grain chemical developers so that, when making enlargements, the finished print does not exhibit the graininess that large "blow-ups" so often produce.

Because of this tendency to graininess and the extreme processing care required, there has been a movement away from the miniature technique by advanced amateurs and professionals. Nevertheless, the miniature still remains an extremely popular camera.

It is especially popular for color photography where, up to recently, it had the field to itself. In the early days of color reproduction, publications accepted 35mm color transparencies without hesitation. Today, very few will do so; color sheet film 4"x5" and larger is now preferred for the technical process of color plate making. Acceptance of 2¼" x 2¼" color transparencies can also be had but the larger size remains the leader in the field of professional color photography.

However, if you are interested in black-and-white and color snapshots for strictly amateur purposes, the miniature camera is for you. Your black-and-white shots, as processed in the U.S., are automatically enlarged to "jumbo" prints (3¼" x 4½"); the color shots are processed by specially equipped commercial laboratories who return the transparencies in the form of cardboard mounted slides* ready for viewing by projection on a large screen or a hand viewer.** When all advantages are weighed, the miniature camera is one of the least expensive precision cameras in use today.

Because it is so economical, it is inexpedient to get an inexpensive (in first cost) miniature camera. There are quite a few cheap ones on the market designed to exploit the popularity of the miniature camera, and these are not good buys because of inferior lens equipment. The small negative size demands the best lens you can afford, one that is fully corrected for color and is sharp to the edges.

To obtain sharp enlargements from a 24x36mm negative is miracle enough without handicapping the process with a lens of poor resolving power. Moreover, you can make a good lens double in brass, if it is removable, by using it in your enlarger, if you do your own enlarging.

For color film, which is much slower than black-and-white film, there will be frequent occasions when you will need lenses of the speed of f/3.5 or faster and composed of complex elements. Such lenses are not cheap but they do enlarge your picture taking possibilities.

Interchangeable Lenses

What adds to the popularity of the miniature camera is the bewildering variety and number of accessories made expressly for its use; the field is simply a paradise as well as a temptation for the gadgeteer.

There is the possibility to purchase additional interchangeable lenses (most better-class miniatures have provision for changing lenses without exposing the film in the camera). Such cameras also have provision for changing viewfinders to accommodate changes in the focal length of the lens employed. The interchangeable lenses come in varying focal lengths — ranging from 28mm (extreme wide-angle) to telephoto lenses of the tremendous magnification of 400mm.

With the wide-angle lens it is possible to take a picture of almost an entire room without having to back up into a wall, a thing it is not possible to do with the standard 50mm lens. The wide-angle lens gives such an extreme depth of field that focusing is almost unnecessary, making the wide-angle lens the ideal lens for "candid" work.

A new wide-angle lens is available whose angle of field is such that it can almost picture more than the human eye can see. As to its depth of field, if the camera is set for a distance of 26 feet and the lens diaphragm at f/11, everything from 5½ feet to infinity will be in sharp focus. That begins to approach the simplicity of the box camera without the disadvantage.

---

*This is now also done for 2¼" x 2¼" color transparencies, hitherto not possible from processors.
**The Polypix Co. 723 S. Wells S., Chicago, offers another service of great interest to 35 mm color fans. From your transparencies they can make enlarged prints (2¾" x 2") with gummed backs in quantities of 100 or more. These can be mounted by the user on his stationery or greeting cards. The result is like expensive color press printing but at a price anyone can afford.

Oddly enough, the extreme opposite: the telephoto lens, can also be used for "candid" work but from another approach. With the telephoto lens, one can take pictures from a great distance and just about fill the negative with a distant scene. This is especially useful for taking picture of subjects to which you cannot approach closely. So it becomes equally useful for taking pictures of a couple on a park bench a hundred yards away or a distant castle that cannot be approached at all. However, it should be noted that with the use of telephoto lenses, camera movement is a grave hazard. It is extremely difficult to get a sharp steady picture with any lens of more than 135 mm focal length without using a tripod.

The miniature camera uses small lengths of 35mm (movie film), in color or black and white. The film comes in two lengths: in rolls of 20 and 36 exposures, when purchased as put up by the film manufacturer. However, it can also be purchased in bulk (100 feet or more), and cut up and loaded in the photographer's dark room. Many who have acquired the necessary dexterity to do this (it is not difficult) are thereby enabled to cut their film cost considerably because the bulk film is quite inexpensive compared to the commercial roll film cartridges.

The usual well-made miniature camera requires many adjustments during picture-taking. This may be trying to an impetuous person, though it spells flexibility for those patient enough to master the adjustments. Certainly, picture-taking is not so simple or fool-proof an operation as with a box camera. On the other hand it escapes the box-camera limitations. Some of the latest models employ reflex focusing through a single lens, diaphragm wide open for brilliant viewing, but with a mechanism which automatically closes the diaphragm to a preset opening when triggered. This is the last word on eliminating the necessity for another movement at the time of shooting. In this category are the new Contaflex, Pentacon, Exacta, Exa, etc.

As an example of the superior possibilities with the miniature camera, it is beginning to share the trend toward 3-D techniques. This added attraction in the use of the miniature camera may easily become the deciding factor in your choice of photographic equipment.

Of course, there have always been cameras capable of photography in the stereoscopic (really 3-D) method. Their disadvantage resided in the fact that, with them, it was not possible to take straight (single) 35mm shots. But now it is possible to purchase an accessory which can be attached to your regular camera; the attachment splits the negative for the spaced, 3-D effect.* And you will still be able to use your camera normally when you desire to do so.

The "stereo-Tach". Produced by Advertising Displays, Inc., Covington, Ky. You might also like the Moller Stereo Viewer Transformer. This is a variable lighting control unit with which the light of your projector can be varied to suit the density of the transparencies.

WHAT EQUIPMENT SHOULD YOU TAKE? 81

The next size larger than the miniature camera is the camera using #127 film; this size produces negatives 1 5/8" x 2 ½". The cameras in this classification are not of sufficient importance or popularity to justify description here.

There is nothing flexibly superior to the 35mm camera with automatic exposure. The last word in convenience.

The Square Format Camera

The next really important size in cameras after the miniature is the format using #120 film to yield negatives 2¼" x 2¼". This film is also employed in cameras yielding 8 negatives 2¼" x 3¼" to a roll of film; those cameras will be dealt with later. In the cameras producing the square negative, the roll produces 12 shots of 2¼" x 2¼" size.

There are some ingenious chaps who can squeeze out 13 shots but the feat is scarcely worth while since the 13th shot may be mutilated or fogged in the processing. With the color #120 roll, which yields only 9 shots,* a tenth shot, also, can be squeezed out but there exists the same hazard of mutilation of the tenth shot.

The 2¼" x 2¼" camera comes in two main divisions: the folding camera and the reflex camera with twin lenses. As in the 35mm field, there are cheap cameras equipped with twin lenses to exploit the popularity of the twin-lens *reflex* camera but which are not true reflex cameras at all. In these psuedo reflex cameras, the upper lens (which should be the focusing lens) is nothing but a glass viewer and it does not focus. These cameras may be good enough for persons who do not expect more from them than what may be accomplished with a box camera. If they know what they are getting, no harm is done.

The reflex (twin-lens) camera is more expensive than the folding type, even when the latter is equipped with a coupled rangefinder. Naturally enough, because the twin-lens camera has an extra lens (for focusing) hardly inferior to the actual taking lens and of good optical quality.

Despite the extra cost, the twin-lens camera enjoys a wide popularity and the popularity increases daily; in fact, there are almost as many twin-lens cameras in use today as miniature cameras. There is good reason for this wide public acceptance.

The best twin-lens cameras almost approach the box camera in simplicity of operation, while retaining the utmost flexibility and precision. The film is transported and the shutter cocked in one fast movement; you see the image in full picture size and focus up to and including the moment of shooting; double exposure (that bugaboo of many cameras) is impossible.

A good camera of this type is as expensive as the best miniature. Film cost is higher too and so is the processing. Thus, 2¼" x 2¼" color slides, mounted in glass, ready to project, will average 25¢ each

---
*The new Ektachrome and Ansco color film yield 12 shots.

against the cost for 35mm cardboard-mounted slides of about 12¢ each. Of course, the 2¼" size is more than twice the size of the 35mm slide and, when projected, needs much less magnification to fill the screen with a large image.

Processing the larger size black and white negative requires less fastidious care; much greater enlargements can be made without running into the graininess that haunts the 35mm worker when making extreme enlargements. If due care is exercised, the 2¼" x 2¼" negative can be enlarged to wall mural size with adequate fidelity.

What makes the high quality twin-lens camera particularly popular with professionals (and amateurs too) is its automatic action on the one hand, because they can work fast with it when needed, and, on the other hand, they are accustomed to composing and judging pictorial values on a ground glass screen. Another advantage of the twin-lens reflex ground glass is that it shows the image rightside up whereas, in the studio cameras, the image on the ground glass back is upside down, requiring a trained eye to judge the composition.

Special Backs

Many photographers (sons of the idle rich, no doubt) make a compromise between the miniature and the twin-lens camera by carrying the former for color and the latter for black and white work. Actually, in the Rolleiflex and Rolleicord twin-lens cameras, there are available accessories whereby this necessity may be avoided. These accessories are a 35mm back and a plate adapter.

With the 35mm back, the camera can use the regular 35mm color film. The back employs a mask with an opening for the 35mm film inside the camera and another mask, for composing and focusing, which is placed on top of the ground glass. The camera then operates normally, with an added provision for counting the exposures of the 35mm film.

These cameras are also probably the only ones of their type to offer the advantage of using individual sheet film holders and ground glass backs as accessories. The use of the plate adapter overcomes the disadvantage of being loaded for black and white when a beautiful color subject presents itself.

By using the adapter one can conveniently switch from black and white to color sheet film. An added advantage is the possibility to use sheet film emulsions not available in roll film. This is no mean advantage; there are some sheet films available that have faster emulsions than any existing roll film, and newer and faster ones are still to come.

Still another advantage afforded by the use of the plate adapter is the possibility to develop individual sheet film as soon as exposed, without the necessity to wait for an entire roll of film to be exposed. When you have a 20-exposure roll of color film, unless you want to waste shots in desperation, the length of time it takes to expose the entire roll may be very trying; the time lapse can even involve the deterioration of the exposures already made.

Candid Techniques with the Reflex Camera

Another reason for the wide use of the reflex camera of the twin-lens type is the manner in which it can be employed in "candid" photography. Though somewhat larger than the 35mm camera, it can be operated in a manner that makes it even less obtrusive than the smaller camera.

The photographer can aim the camera at his objective, while apparently looking in another direction, meanwhile focusing in the ground glass as usual. It takes a bit of practice to judge the image that way but, once the facility is acquired, much can be photographed that would otherwise be impossible; the subjects being photographed are completely disarmed and unsuspicious.

You can use the same technique for taking pictures of persons in back of you. Do not look backwards; merely let your camera look backwards while, you, looking forwards, can study the image and shoot when you wish. The subject will never know he was shot.

Likewise, you can take a picture over the heads of a crowd. You hold the camera over your head, camera upside down, ground glass nearest you, and you can then focus as well as in a normal position. You use the camera almost as though it were a periscope. But you had better shoot at not less than 1/100 second to avoid camera shake.

The Folding Camera

As you get into the larger sizes, the attempt is made to save bulk and for this purpose the folding type camera is most frequently used. This can range from the #120 film to postcard size and beyond. Usually the postcard size is the upper limit though some "oldies" used even larger film material. The folding type cameras do not usually employ coupled rangefinders, though some of the lenses used are excellent. The folding type camera, for large film sizes, is not as common as it used to be. In the $2\frac{1}{4}''$ x $3\frac{1}{4}''$ size there exists a Speed Graphic (press type) camera but, in the opinion of many, a camera of its complexity is better suited to its larger brothers in the $3\frac{1}{4}''$ x $4\frac{1}{4}''$ and $4''$ x $5''$ sizes.

The Larger Cameras

In the $3\frac{1}{4}''$ x $4\frac{1}{4}''$ and the $4''$ x $5''$ sizes, you are getting into the bulkier but very useful sizes. Unless you sell your pictures, prints in this size avoid necessity for enlargements; are large enough for all practical viewing purposes for the amateur. Most of the cameras made in those sizes are known as press-type cameras, so called because they are so popular with press photographers. The most widely used for press work are the Speed Graphic and Graflex cameras. Folding cameras using the same sizes of film can sometimes be found with tropical construction, which is usually a wood that resists corrosion. Such cameras will be of European make and have been scarce recently.

The Graflex, with its revolving back, large ground glass screen, automatic diaphragm (in one model); the Graphic, with its adjustable front, extension bellows, choice of focal plane or between-lens shutters, choice of sheet film; these are widely favored by serious photographers and professionals. The cameras have great flexibility in operation and their results, when used with good lenses, have won prizes all over the world. Were it not for their bulk and weight, they would be the ideal all-purpose camera. Alas, one has to be in good physical condition to lug them around and, for the traveler, their bulk constitutes a serious handicap.

The Speed Graphic, used so much in newspaper photography, can be whipped into action as fast as any "candid" camera by skilled operators. Incidentally, there is available for cameras of this size the fastest film made, with a conservative rating of ASA 400. With forced development, this rating can actually be increased to double that amazing figure. However, the average person reading this book may not find that fact of great significance, it being outside the scope of his requirements.

The Graflex camera is, of course, one of the prime reflex cameras in existence; it has an old and honored history. It is not as popular as it once was but I don't know of any serious photographer who hasn't yearned to have one at some time. Its great disadvantage is its bulk; it is huge!

Polaroid-Land Camera

This is a maverick in the field — there is no other like it in the world. Its sales, increasing almost at a geometric rate, threaten to make mavericks of the conventional cameras. It is the camera which produces, by its own internal processing, a picture while you wait — the actual picture, not a negative. It can produce a finished print, contact size of course, in 1 minute.

Its owners are dazzled by the prospect of astonishing the beholders, and themselves, by whipping out a finished print, and in a good size too, in so short a time. It seems impossible to fail with this camera because you can see the results at once and can shoot over again immediately afterwards if results are not satisfactory. Also the problem of processing is completely eliminated. (A boon when traveling!)

You do not need a developing tank, paper, chemicals; nor do you need a dark room. Enlargements are possible but not on the spot. They are obtainable from the Polaroid Co. only.

FILM AND ACCESSORIES

With film, you run up against the import limitations imposed by most foreign countries. In theory, you are not allowed to bring in more than 2 rolls of black and white film, one roll of color film, and a dozen sheet film. Actually, I've brought in considerably more than that amount on many occasions, especially color film, and have never had any trouble about it. The customs inspectors are given considerable discretion, especially in their interpretation of "reasonable" amount (as allowed under the usual regulations), and I know of no American with legitimate activity who has had any difficulty.

However, to reassure those tourists who are timid about official regulations (which are listed elsewhere), let me say that film for all the sizes of cameras described here is available in most countries. This is especially true in Europe where most of the film produced by native manufacturers is equal in quality to the best of ours — some of it is world-famous. In any case, there are few foreign countries where you will not find a Kodak agency, with a complete line of Kodak products.

There will be some difficulty about getting color film, even in the popular roll-film sizes. European-made color film, however, will probably be available but it is not the same as Kodachrome or Ansco film and there may be difficulty in getting it processed in the U.S., if you bring it back for processing.*

The difficulty in getting color film has been widely complained about by travelers. I have been frequently asked about this situation. In the first place, the situation is improving. More Eastman and Ansco agencies are now scattered throughout the world than formerly, and they stock a limited supply of the color film in use in the U.S. In the second place, you can safely bring in more color film than the usual customs regulations allow if, obviously, the quantity is not great enough to anticipate the possibility that the film might be for resale for profit. One of my acquaintances brought into and transported through Europe 75 rolls of 35mm Kodachrome without encountering any difficulty. However, such a quantity does tempt fate.

---

*The General Photo Supply Co., 136 Charles St., Boston 14, Mass. offers to process any color film made anywhere. This laboratory can handle negative and positive material and can make color prints by any color process.

Kurt Mayer Color Labs, 49 W. 27 St., New York, also processes all foreign color film, as well as British and French Kodachrome, which give better effects when specially handled, the colors being more delicate than the domestic color film.

Film Comes in Numerous Varieties

Film is the camera's vitamin. It goes without saying that it isn't the camera which makes the picture — it's the film inside the camera. The camera is the tool but the film is the actual vehicle. The average person takes film so much for granted that he never stops to analyze what a chemical miracle film really is.

In the main, it consists of a base (cellulose acetate) carrying on its surface uncountable numbers of silver bromide crystals; these are light-sensitive and, when exposed to light, turn black; it is these minute crystals which, in varied and complex patterns, form the actual image.

Film is manufactured in many varieties because no single kind is ideal for all purposes; that is, speaking of black and white film.* Color film involves a widely different manufacturing and processing technique from black and white film and is offered in much fewer varieties than the latter. When the photographer has to make a decision about what kind of color film to use, he does not have to make a profound study before making the decision; there is not a great deal of choice.

So far as black and white film is concerned, the average photographer can confine his choice to the two main varieties: orthochromatic and panchromatic. These varieties, in turn, are subdivided by speed. By speed is meant the speed with which the emulsion reacts to exposure to light. It must be noted that speed is gained at a cost in tonal range and graininess, the slower speed film being superior in both qualities. When film with wide tonal range and moderate graininess is employed, enlargements of great magnification can be made satisfactorily. The faster film's tonal range is more compressed and extreme enlargements will be grainy.

Since the foregoing was written, some of the well-known film manufacturers have come out with film doubling and, under certain conditions**, tripling, the speed of the hitherto fastest film such as Super XX or Superpan Press types.

Film manufacturers have been in a competitive race in this matter. Future experience in the hands of photographers will indicate whether film quality and workability have been sacrificed in this race for fast film emulsions.

One manufacturer has been confident enough to claim in public announcements that there has been no increase in graininess (such as becomes evident in considerable enlargement) in the characteristics of the new film. Wonderful if true.

One of these remarkable new fast films is announced as an import from England. It comes in the three popular roll film sizes: 35 mm, 620, & 120. Usually, the ultra fast film has been available only in sheet film, such as is used by professionals. Roll film brings faster working into the hands of the amateur.

---
*See table suggesting what film might be chosen for various subjects—Page 87.
**Depending on kind of developer and length & development.

The unusual feature of this latest film, produced by one of the famous manufacturers of the world, is its speed. It is rated at 400 ASA (daylight), and 160 Tungsten. Moreover, it is altogether likely that with forced development, these speeds could be increased.

While the film is declared to be of medium contrast, there need be no doubt that the contrast could be increased, too, by appropriate exposure and development technique, familiar to photographers who do their own processing. The claim is also made that there is no increase in grain, that bugaboo of high speed film.

The orthochromatic film (ortho, for short) would be a logical choice where sensitivity to blue and green is desired and where its relative insensitivity to red is no handicap. The latter quality makes ortho film a good choice for night shots and for shooting with the regular flash bulbs. Also, its use is a great convenience for amateur processors because the film can be developed by inspection under a red or amber safelight; this inspection guides the processor in the matter of length of development, since the development time can be altered to suit given situations. Panchromatic film has to be developed in total darkness and therefore development time cannot be altered for film which has been badly exposed.

Where sensitivity to all colors is required, panchromatic film becomes the logical choice and the speed of the film you choose can be decided by the kind of shooting you're going to do. If you're going to do much action stuff, Tri-X might be chosen for its extreme speed, at some sacrifice in enlargement possibilities. All panchromatic film, *regardless of the speed chosen,* must be developed in total darkness.

Guide to Choosing Black and White Film

Subject	*Film*
Outdoors, Landscapes, People, daylight or late afternoon	Ortho or Panchro
Outdoors, Landscapes, People, early in the day or bright light	Panchro
Outdoors, bright light, early day — people, action, interiors, with existing light	Fast panchro
Flash shots, interiors Sea and sky, landscapes (where cloud effects desired)	Ortho or panchro — slow or fast

Color film is as easy to use as black and white film. The same camera that takes black and white pictures can take color pictures, providing the lens is of good quality and is corrected for color. The only limiting factor is speed. Color film has about one-tenth the speed of fast black and white film.

Amateur photographers are losing their timidity about color film. They no longer show hesitancy about departing from the rigid confines of manufacturers' specifications. Thus, many have discovered that there are advantages to using daylight color film at night and nighttime film in daylight.

They are experimenting, too, with colored artificial lighting. One of the interesting new tricks is the use of daylight color film to give the effect of moonlight, by the use of blue filters over the lens, and with varying exposures.

All these experiments use up money in film cost but few enthusiastic amateurs are deterred by that consideration.

If you want to take color pictures, a fast lens is an essential, unless you want to restrict yourself to artificial lighting and lengthy exposures. It would certainly be advisable to employ a lens with a diaphragm of not less than f/4.5. If you could confine yourself to color picture-taking on bright days only, outdoors, f/6.3 might be good enough, but who wants to limit himself that way, apart from the fact that an f/6.3 lens is usually not of the first quality.

Filters and Other Accessories

Generally, the kind of accessories you are likely to find useful enough to take along are neither bulky nor extensive. You really can get along with only one filter, unless you are after and are competent to produce special effects.

The medium-yellow filter is a good compromise for most purposes. With the exercise of a little judgment in exposure, you can increase or decrease its potential. Many photographers keep it on their cameras constantly, when shooting outdoors, allowing for the increase in exposure its use makes necessary.

What the yellow filter does is to hold back its complementary color, which is the blue of the sky or any other blueish tone existing in the scene being photographed; film is most sensitive to blue and if left uncorrected would register on the film out of proportion to its actual tone value as seen by the eye. When a yellow filter is employed with panchromatic film, the result is closer to the values seen by our eyes and clouds have a better chance to register on the negative.

Deep yellow, orange, and red filters go further in this respect and, with their use, you can even distort the values for dramatic effects. However, such distorted effects are not always pleasing; the average person will find more pleasing the effects obtained by the slight correction afforded with the use of the medium-yellow filter.

The medium-yellow (#2) filter also serves to reduce haze and render distant objects more clearly when shooting long mountain vistas. It is well to keep in mind that the film "sees" these long vistas less clearly than the eye does and you'll be surprised what a difference the filter can make in the finished result in such situations.

Do not use a yellow filter with color film; for technical reasons too lengthy to explain here, they are not compatible. While advanced amateurs are experimenting with the use of filters with color film—either filters mounted on artificial lights, or mounted on the camera lens—the average person had best confine himself to the use of a filter known as a haze filter. This filter serves to pierce atmospheric haze (in mountain shots, particularly) and its use does not require any increase in exposure time.

For black and white film there are filters called sky filters in which the upper half of the filter is yellow, and the lower half of the filter is clear, or graduated towards clearness. This filter, also, does not make it necessary to increase exposure time since its main purpose is merely to hold back the sky while giving normal exposure to the main part of the landscape which is covered by the clear glass only. This filter might also serve as a haze filter for black and white film, though a regular yellow filter might be considered more satisfactory.

A useful little accessory is a device providing for delayed action of the shutter. The Germans, from whom a great deal of such auxiliary devices are derived, call it "Auto-Knips"; it is also manufactured in the U.S. It can be employed on any camera which has provision for a cable release, with which it is easiest to operate, and it permits the snapping of the shutter about 10 seconds after you trigger it. This lapse of time allows the photographer himself to get into the picture before the shutter snaps. Of course, to do this, it is necessary that the camera be mounted on a tripod or some other solid support. A cable release is also useful for snapping the shutter at all times; it serves to eliminate the jar (and resulting camera shake) when snapping the shutter. Cable releases are usually 5-8 inches long but there are cable releases made for remote operation that can be several feet long. There is one such available, called the Kagra Remote Control Extension unit, that is greatly superior in operating convenience to the "Auto Knips." With the latter, there ensues a scramble by the nimble-footed (and those not so nimble) to get oneself into position and tranquilly posed within the allowable ten seconds. That makes for pictures that reveal nervestrain.

The Kagra, with two lengths of tubing, a bulb to squeeze, and a metal connector to the camera shutter, allows one to get into position and composed and relaxed. There is a world of time, completely at your disposal. The bulb can be left on the ground and stepped on to take the picture or held behind one's back and squeezed when ready.

Further, the 33 foot length allows one to set up the camera and take close-up shots of birds, animals, and other wildlife from a suitable distance so that one's physical presence does not alarm the subjects. If the camera shutter is synchronized, the Kagra can also be used to trigger the shutter for flash photography from a distance.

Exposure Meter Techniques

There are few photographers, today, taking their hobby seriously, who fail to provide themselves with a modern exposure meter. If you could be certain of taking only black and white pictures, of average subjects, and in bright daylight, you could probably dispense with an exposure meter after memorizing a few basic rules about exposures for the particular film you are going to use. (See "Basic Exposures", page 118).

There are some photographers, in a position to choose their own conditions, who have standardized on a formula for the exposure of one favorite film under the set conditions that, in their experience, will give them just the results they want. These photographers can and do dispense with an exposure meter.

But there are so many variable conditions within a single day that it is rarely possible to do such casual shooting. Even experts can be fooled by quick changes in lighting and contrasts.

This problem of variability is nuisance enough when using black and white film, whose latitude is such that you can over- or under-expose 3 to 4 times and still be able to get a printable negative. The emphasis is on *printable*—that does not mean a perfect negative.

But when using color film, the problem of exposure is compounded. Color film is so much slower on the one hand, and its latitude is negligible, on the other hand. To make matters worse, inaccurate exposure in color work is immediately noticeable by anyone whereas, in black and white work, perfect exposure is not so easily judged and can often be a matter of personal opinion.

Suffice it to say that an exposure meter will, in the hands of the average photographer, pay off in the saving of wasted film and in proccessing costs. Besides, when a tourist is armed with an exposure meter he will have the added assurance that he will not have wasted his once-in-a-lifetime opportunity for exotic pictures. He need only balance the cost of an exposure meter against the cost of his foreign transportation to determine relative values.

For the photographer who does his own processing on panchromatic film, an exposure meter becomes an indispensable tool for providing negatives of uniform density. Since panchromatic film must be developed in perfect darkness and there's no opportunity to increase or decrease development time to accord with the density of individual negatives, uniformity of negative density can only be assured by uniformity of exposures; to obtain uniform exposures is essentially the property of the exposure meter.

Generally, in the purchase of an exposure meter, the manufacturer's manual of instructions accompanies the instrument to enable the beginner to make the best use of exposure meter technique. The beginner should be advised—and the manual probably does this—that even the most elaborate of instruments (in fact, *especially* with them) the exposure readings require interpretation in use.

One of the most important rules to remember in this connection is that, with subjects having great light contrast, the exposure to be used should be a compromise between the extreme light reading and the extreme dark reading of the light reflected from the subject. To ascertain this properly, it is necessary to get close enough to hold the meter within a few feet or less of the subject to be photographed.

An interesting device may be employed when you cannot get close enough to a subject to get an accurate meter reading. Hold a medium-gray cardboard at arm's-length and take an exposure reading of it. That reading would approximate the exposure to be used. This technique is based on two assumptions: (1) That the subject to be photographed is in the same light as the grey card you're reading; (2) That the subject to be photographed is an average one. Most subjects will average middle-gray values over-all.

This technique should be used only with black and white film. Color film, being more critical and having less latitude, presents more possibility for error and therefore this technique will yield only approximate results.

Use an exposure that lies somewhere in between the extreme readings. The exposure could be halfway between, or you can favor one area over another, depending on which you're most concerned with. When you take the readings, incidentally, it would be a good idea to point the meter slightly downward toward the subject to avoid some of the sky light which will give a false reading.

If you are an advanced amateur photographer with a scientific turn of mind, you might like to make a series of test exposures, with the meter as a guide, against the operation of your camera before you go off on a long trip.

Your lens and shutter, particularly the latter, may have some individual characteristics and by these tests you may discover what modifications, if any, you may need to make from the manufacturer's recommendations, for your particular set-up. Or the tests may disclose some shutter defects which might need repair before you leave.

Exposure meters that are equipped with photoelectric cells are delicate instruments and should be handled with as much care as you would use in handling an expensive camera. There are a few makes that are reputed to be shockproof but I wouldn't care to test the claim.

Nor would I suggest the attempt to repair a meter that had been dropped and its function impaired. It's not worth the effort and there could be no confidence in a meter that had been repaired.

All the foregoing may be ignored by the fortunate photographer armed with the last word in cameras, cameras equipped with the automatic exposure device. Coupled to the shutter to give the exposure, these mechanisms almost make photography ultra-simple. Experts still prefer to use judgment in addition but automatic exposure has been a godsend to the average person.

Carry-All Case

It might add considerably to your convenience in traveling, and on photo excursions, to get a bag which will carry all your equipment: camera, accessories, and film. These bags are not only of value for their convenience in transportation but they serve to protect your equipment against damage.

Photo shops have bags that are specially made for this purpose, with divided compartments for the various articles. Usually, these bags are made with a shoulder strap so they can be carried out of your way and leave you free for any other activity.

Should You Use a Tripod?

Here we come to a "fielder's choice"—you may or may not wish to be burdened with a tripod. Ordinary snapshooters do not use one. On the other hand, their pictures reflect the deficiency in the form of fuzzy pictures due to camera movement. This is true not only of the pictures taken with the ubiquitous box camera (whose shutter is generally fixed at 1/25 second) but poor light often compels that same slow speed in cameras boasting faster shutters.

Many of the interesting places you'll be visiting are inside buildings, galleries, museums, castles, cathedrals, town halls, picturesque taverns. In such places, even with a fast lens, the available light might demand longer exposures; often time exposures.

Even photographic novices know that this calls for the use of a tripod. Anything slower than 1/25 second exposure cannot be hand-held with any certainty of success. I have made fairly steady exposures at a full second but it was pushing my luck.

Of course, it may be necessary to get permission to use a tripod inside the building to be visited. Especially is this true of museums whose directors are prepared for the request to make an exception to the general rule.

In some of the public parks of Europe, you may find it necessary to pay a small fee for permission to use a tripod. Another complication exists in the fact that the use of a tripod stamps the user as a professional. Not only does this make the average person shy away from you but it might make you come under police regulations respecting commercial photography.

It would be well to inquire from local people in the know (photo shops would be a prime source of information) about the regulations concerning the use of tripods in the region and whether a police permit is required. When that proves to be the case, the permit is not difficult to get but the necessity is a nuisance.

It is alway advisable, indoors or outdoors, and wherever the public moves or gathers, to make use of the tripod in a manner that causes no hindrance to the free movement of whatever traffic exists.

In any case, take no tripod at all rather than the flimsy ones that can be found at temptingly cheap prices. If you're going to use one, get one with sturdy legs, collapsible for packing but not in action, and with tips that will hold the ground and not slip at a puff of wind. Get one whose mounting head sets quickly in all directions, requiring the fewest time-consuming adjustments. There's an excellent one that meets all these requirements—any photo shop will recognize it by these specifications.

Its manufacturer* also makes a carrying case for the tripod. The carrying case is made of durable leather and it is equipped with a zipper fastening along its entire length. The tripod can be collapsed into the bag, which is then zipped up, and the whole thing can be slung over one's shoulder and thus be carried with the least inconvenience and bulk.

Another convenient support, though not as satisfactory as a regular tripod, is known as the Unipod. It consists of a single pole which is collapsible and which extends from 35" to 60". It is very light in weight and it has very little bulk—but it's only a compromise.

Another camera support, excellent both for convenience and flexibility, is the Kodak Flexiclamp. It is small, can be carried in a jacket pocket. Its most valuable feature is that it can be fastened securely on to any piece of furniture, door, pole, or bench that is handy—in fact, anything that is sturdy and stationary. It has a regular tripod socket for holding the camera and a swivel joint so that the camera can be moved around in any direction. It is an excellent substitute for a tripod in most places. Even in an open field, you might be able to find a tree branch that could take the clamp and serve your purpose.

If you are compelled to dispense with a tripod while traveling, it is still possible to take pictures with relatively long exposures by setting the camera up on a fence, post, wall, a window, or table, or while resting your camera on a knee while seated. Anything that will hold the camera steady will do. As a further assurance against jarring the camera you could use a cable release—use the longest one possible.

These precautions are really necessary; with the greatest care in the world it is still not possible to take a long exposure and release the shutter with finger pressure without shaking the camera. There are chaps with nerves so steady that they can hold a camera steady for

---

*Quick-Set, Inc., 8121 Central Park Ave., Stokie, Ill.

exposures up to a full second (which is the longest possible without resorting to a time exposure); but they have their failures and, for the average photographer, long exposures without a camera support are not advisable.

Lens Tissue

Another useful thing to have with you is a camel's hair brush to remove dirt from the camera, inside and out. For cleaning the lens use nothing but soft lens tissue. A convenient book of these can be obtained in photo shops. A little cleansing fluid on the tissue will help; get only the kind of fluid that is recommended for the purpose. And polish gently; remember, lenses are made of optical glass, which is delicate and easily injured.

Is Your Equipment in Perfect Condition?

While the condition of your equipment is not very important at home, where repair facilities are at your convenient command, the matter becomes a major problem abroad and if it cannot be solved, it could ruin your trip.

Therefore, it is advisable, if there is any doubt about the condition of your equipment, that you have it checked before leaving on your trip. Repairs *can* be made abroad—I've had frequent occasion for them—but reliability cannot be taken for granted. This is not said to impugn the honor of repair mechanics in foreign countries, but, after all, you are a transient customer and it's unlikely that they will be called to account for irresponsible work.

If you must have repairs made during the course of your trip, the local tourist office is not always a reliable guide in the matter. Again, the local camera club is a far better guide. If no camera club exists, ask a professional photographer.

The average photo shop is not always set up for repair work, though it will not hesitate to take it on. Or it may "farm out" the job to someone who can do the work. The trick is to find that chap yourself. Of course, I'm speaking of elaborate or expensive equipment—anyone can repair a box camera—if it's worth repairing.

CAMERA "BUYS" IN FOREIGN COUNTRIES

Many wives complain (mine leads the host) that their husbands spend more time in camera shops abroad than they do sightseeing. It is a valid complaint. The fact is that some European countries offer great bargains in photographic equipment for the person who is familiar with photo values.

Of course, shopping for such equipment had best be confined to the industrialized countries where the manufacture of such equipment is of suitable quality. One could not expect to buy a well-made piece of optical equipment in a backward country, for example.

Germany is, of course, *the* country for the purchase of the highest quality in photographic equipment and it supplies the greatest bargains; other European countries trail not too far behind. Some of the finest cameras in the world are imported into the U.S. from Germany; to list them all would fill a sizeable book but here are a few of the better-known makes:

CAMERAS
Zeiss Contax
Zeiss Contessa Nettal
Zeiss Ikoflex
Zeiss Ikonta (in various models)
Leica
Rolleiflex and Rolleicord
Baldina (various models)
Voigtlander Prominent
Voigtlander Vito (various models)
Voigtlander Dynamatic
Voigtlander Bessa
Voigtlander Perkeo
Exacta (miniature & standard)
Linhof Technika
Retina (various models)
Agfa

MOVIE CAMERAS
Nizo (tops)
Agfa
Zeiss Movikon
Siemens

PROJECTORS
Siemens
Ditmar
Agfa
Nizo

EXPOSURE METERS
Actino
Sixtomat
Ikophot

ENLARGERS
Leitz Focomat
Viegel Exact 66

The German photo dealer* knows his field inside out; he is reliable and you can rely on his advice. Anything you buy in Germany will

---

**The largest photo dealer in the world is Photo-Porst, Karolinenstrasse 3, Nurenberg. The establishment is a veritable treasure-house of photographic apparatus and of bargains.*

cost from 33% to 50% less than the same instrument costs in the U.S. This is based on the assumption that anything you buy will be included in your personal exemption from duty as a tourist when you return to the U.S.

Accessories and film are equally attractive buys. *Peromnia* film is one of the best in Germany and is worthy of the attention of the most meticulous photographer. Cost: 33% less than in the U.S. for similar film. And there are fantastic photographic bargains for American dollars in East Germany, if you can get in. It is not difficult nor hazardous for American tourists to get in or out of East Berlin where the great bargains prevail. Tourists who behave with circumspection are not molested.

Switzerland and Italy are the next bargain counters; England, France, and Austria trailing. Italy and Switzerland both offer a very high quality 35mm camera: Italy's *Rectaflex,* Switzerland's *Alpa.* Italy also offers a good range of other cameras as well, the Ferrania being a good name in both cameras and film.

Switzerland is also the home of the finest amateur movie equipment in the world: the famous Bolex line.

France produces some well-made 35mm and larger size cameras; those equipped with the famous Berthiot lenses equal any in the world. And they are gradually improving the French version of the twin-lens camera to the point where it is becoming a formidable rival to the established cameras of this type in the world market. Nevertheless, French equipment is no bargain; prices closely approach those prevailing in the U.S. for comparable products.

There are many photographers who praise British-made photographic products. Indeed, some of the British cameras are quite ingenious and have a world reputation. Names like Selfix, Soho, Ross, Ilford, Dallmeyer, and Taylor-Hobson are about as well known throughout the world as the name Kodak. Ilford has produced the fastest known film* and is a leading innovator in the manufacture of fine photographic papers.

However, I would not consider British apparatus superior to ours in quality and no advantage is offered in price. On the other hand, you might possibly find a British piece of equipment with an ingenious feature that you might like.

A country that is certainly far away for most Americans but which today offers some amazing photo bargains is Japan. Japan has recently invaded the U.S. with some very fine cameras, in both the 35mm and twin-lens types. Within each category, there are few cameras superior to Japan's Nikon, Canon, Konica, Koniflex, and Mamiya. In Japan, these cameras would probably cost the tourist one-half what they cost

---

DuPont has a new sheet film that may rival it.

in the U.S. Even in the U.S., these cameras sell at prices that are lower than the cameras they compete with. These bargains in the U.S. will last only as long as necessary for the Japanese cameras to establish themselves solidly. Users of these cameras have sent me some very enthusiastic letters about their performance and report themselves highly pleased.

There is one difficulty about the purchase of the best of these instruments, in both Germany and Japan: they are difficult to get. The reason is that the manufacturers supply the native shops with the very minimum quantity of the particular instruments which are in great demand in other countries. The country most favored for exportation of these products is the U.S. Thus, if a German manufacturer can sell to the U.S. and get dollars, he will favor export rather than domestic sales.

As an example of the kind of difficulty you may run into, I will relate a personal experience. In Germany, two years ago, I had to scour a half dozen cities before I could purchase a Rolleiflex. I was only able to get one finally because the dealer from whom it was obtained was under obligation to me and jumped my order over a long waiting list for the one Rollei he had received in six months of back ordering. However, he informed me that this difficulty did not exist in the case of other cameras that were not in such demand in the U.S. even though they were considered excellent in their respective fields. You can walk into any shop and secure at once any Zeiss, Voigtlander, Retina, Exacta, or Leica model.

When purchasing photographic apparatus in a foreign country be sure to get a bill of sale. Dealers (and not only the dealers in photograghic equipment) will ask whether you want the bill made out for an amount less than the sum you actually have to pay; presumably it's a good idea to present such a bill at the American customs department. Well, it's not a good idea; the only person it fools is yourself. American customs officials know values as well as any experts in the world. Have the bill made out legitimately; that's better all around. The exemption from duty for tourists is so liberal that there's no reason for subterfuge.

You might be tempted by the photographic bargains in the countries mentioned to buy a camera for the purpose of resale in the U.S. That way you could make a little profit and reduce the cost of your trip. Many tourists have thought to do this but the plan will not be successful.

You must know that there is a provision in our customs regulations which prohibits the resale of any item purchased abroad on which duty had not been paid; which, in short, you had brought into the country duty-free under your tourist exemption.

The prohibition extends for a period of three years on photographic equipment. At the end of that time, you are free to sell or trade the equipment without any limitations. But, you will note, that means the equipment will have had three years of depreciation even if it had not been used; frequent changes in style and mechanism make for a high degree of obsolescence in photographic equipment so the chances are that if you attempt to carry out the original plan you will not even get your own money back.

It is inadvisable to attempt to evade this regulation by trading your camera anyway, on the assumption that the authorities will never know. It happens that the photographic industry is a closely regulated one. Dealers are obliged to report to authorities any equipment presented to them for trade or sale whose serial number is not registered as coming into the country through regular trade channels.

The fact that it is unlawful to sell a camera purchased abroad for three years should make you cautious about the camera you buy. You must be fairly sure it's exactly the instrument you want because if it is not, you're going to be stuck with it for a fairly long time. I'm sure wives will welcome the provision; it might keep husbands from going off half-cocked and buying everything in sight in the attractive photo shop windows.

ARE YOU TRAVELING WITH A MOVIE CAMERA?

This section will deal only with 8mm and 16mm movie equipment. 35mm movies are strictly a professional proposition from all angles, from picture-taking to processing. If you were to use 35mm equipment, you would be classified as a professional and, in many countries, you would find yourself thrust into complications that it would be best to avoid.

Movie-making, even in amateur film sizes, is not a cheap hobby; it's a luxury by any criterion. But it happens to be one which, undeterred, great numbers of ordinary folk embrace with enthusiasm. As a result, it bulks large in the photographic industry, forming a constantly increasing percentage of its annual volume.

Families with young children, especially, find the movie camera an indispensable means of recording the growth of their children and the records so collected make a graphic and nostalgic addition to their lives.

Indispensable, also, is the movie camera when it comes to recording the many bewildering travel experiences which only viewing in retrospect can properly help one to digest and to store in one's memory. While a still camera "freezes" a split-second segment of life, the movie camera preserves a fluid and moving record that is more dynamic and heartfelt.

It furnishes a touch of Hollywood magic that is under your own control; your own movie impinges on your life in a way that Hollywood can never do; and it can do this as frequently as you like and at your own convenience. These advantages are enough to outweigh the cost for many for whom the home movie is an engrossing interest.

You cannot do your own film processing, and you should be glad that this is so. You could not begin to assemble the machinery necessary for the purpose nor would it be worth your while to attempt to equal the processing techniques of the manufacturer's laboratory.

Apparently, then, all the amateur movie-maker has to do is to press the button and to shoot what lies before him. And, in many cases, alas, that is exactly what he does do.

The beginner generally slings his camera in front of some foreign scene and arranges to have a member of his party slowly walk towards him; with the scene as a background, he grinds away at the "action." He fully anticipates that he has captured a dynamic record of the scene. All that he is doing, really, is to duplicate what thousands of other tourists have done before him. Or what another traveler with a still camera might do. The results in either case are stilted.

Movie lab people can tell you that this procedure is followed by 75% of movie-making travelers. It bores the lab people stiff to process the stuff and, it may be expected, will also bore the friends to whom the pictures will be shown and who will wish, before they are finished, that the projector would go out of commission.

To get pictures that will be out of the usual run and will reward both the taking and the showing, it's a good plan to plot your action in advance from a basic idea that will create the necessary interest. Use the professional technique of distant view, followed by middle distance shot, then close-ups; and change the various bits of action to suit the changes in perspective.

An over-all view of a distant castle is less interesting, however necessary it might be for the record, then a close-up view of a member of your party examining a small part of it, while at the same time the custodian points to it in an attitude of explanation. That would be action with relevancy and meaning. Or take a dramatic view of someone leaning down from the tower engaged in conversation, with gestures, while you shoot up from below, as though you are merely an observer. Sometimes, scenes like these arrange themselves spontaneously; sometimes you have to stage them.

The custodians in some remote places are interesting characters in themselves and will cooperate to stage anything you might want to do. Very cooperative, that is, for a small tip, and they will turn handsprings for a good one.

If your camera is ideal for picturing the pleasant parts of your trip it is equally valuable for picturing the unpleasant parts. Everything combines to make a trip, both sunshine and rain. And, while the disagreeable incidents may irritate at the moment of their happening, they will lend a touch of grim humor after the event—plus the interest.

Though your camera is designed to show action, it is not designed to create action; that is, it should not contribute action in the form of camera shake. Camera movement in a movie camera is, if anything, more disagreeable than in a still camera. So never, unless a special effect is intended, "pan" your movie camera: move it sideways or up and down. The result of such movement, on the screen, when added to the action you *wish* to record, will be very disconcerting to the viewer and will produce more fatigue than interest in your audience.

You may come across a fairly large scene which can be shot only from a fixed and distant spot—one that does not permit close-ups. That contingency presents one of the few justifications for "panning." If you have to pan, do so very slowly, without jerky movement. Allow at least six seconds for each small section, overlapping as you go along. Remember, it takes the eye a little time to register an impression.

Are You Traveling With A Movie Camera? 101

There are three speeds available in the average movie camera: 8 frames per second (slow speed); 16 frames per second (normal speed); and 32 frames per second (fast speed)*.

However take note that the fast camera speed makes the action appear slow and the slow camera speed makes the action appear fast. A thorough knowledge of this principle will enable the movie-maker to accomplish trick effects. Possibly, the manufacturer's manual of instructions will suggest some of the tricks possible by utilizing this principle. There are cameras in the 16mm size that afford continuously variable speed; very useful but tricky.

Close-ups are the most dramatic effects possible, always more interesting than normal shots. If there is a limit to the closeness of range afforded by your camera, you can get supplementary lenses that will reduce the minimum distance afforded by your camera. There are supplementary lenses that will enable you to take pictures of objects within a few *inches* of your lens.

When taking close-ups, use your exposure meter to measure the light falling on your subject. Be careful not to let your shadow fall on the subject while using the meter; that would give you a false reading. On distant shots, you have to content yourself with an exposure based on the general light prevailing rather than that which is available on any specific portion of the scene.

For titles, shoot some of the signposts you will see, not only to identify the spot but to add their own touch of picturesqueness. When picturing such a still object, give it enough time to register: three to four seconds at least.

While using a signpost for a title is such a good idea that it cannot be overworked, it could be made still more interesting if you could include in the scene a native pointing the way (to where you want to go, apparently), or giving a direction to a member of your party, or contributing any other piece of action in connection with the signpost that you might conceive.

For example: Who will soon forget the scene in the movie *From Here to Eternity* when the camera pans from the figures sprawled in the roadway to the road signs pointing to "Pearl Harbor—8 Miles"! The road sign indicated in this manner became a pivot around which revolved the dramatic turning-point of the story. Use your imagination to develop constructive ideas like this.

Since, as in still photography, dates are important, try to photograph something that discloses the date: a calendar inside a quaint country store would be ideal. Or the license plate of an automobile which may not only show the yearly date but may also picture a foreign make of car. If you take other trips in the future, the date is useful to establish the logical sequence of events or to avoid confusion with later trips.

There are movie cameras with additional speeds.

When the film is being processed, you could instruct the lab to make a duplicate of the date section and, by splicing that duplicate into the beginning of the film, combining it with the title, the date becomes a sort of title too.

As you get further along in the movie-making hobby, you'll be observing theatre movies with greater intensity and taking note of some of the Hollywood tricks of the trade and begin to make use of them yourself—at least you'll be able to adapt the simpler ones.

There are many commercial outfits that produce finished movie subjects for home projection—they are on sale at photo shops. Among these professionally produced movies for home use there will undoubtedly be scenes which you may have visited on your own trip. It's a simple matter to splice some of these scenes into your own reels to produce greater verisimilitude to your collection and to enhance the all-round interest.*

If you find the title schemes of such professional films more interesting than your own they could be spliced in to substitute for yours or, perhaps, combined with yours. Splicing is no great trick and, if done with ingenuity, can produce marvelously integrated results. Properly done, the splicing will not be noticed in projection. To do it properly means that you have to make sure to match the spliced sections in tone quality whether color or black and white.

Color movies are so much more exciting than black and white that, to most people, they are worth the extra cost. They do not double the cost as many people suppose, not quite. Moreover, in the small, easily-carried 8mm movie camera, and the small projector made for that size, color cost is so moderate that many completely ignore black and white altogether and confine their movie-making to color alone.

Home movie-making has broadened considerably with the advent of synchronized sound, whether on tape or wire. This development brings home movie-making almost into equality with Hollywood entertainment.

Of course, the amateur can never complete with the professional in sheer sophisticated technique. But the amateur has one decisive advantage; his film reflects his own life, his own family, and pictures his own friends—something Hollywood cannot hope to do.

Not only does sound combined with movies† constitute a heavy extra expense, it is scarcely a practical proposition for the average photog-

---

*Castle Films (a company producing such film) lists: "Africa Untamed;" "Simba—Killer-Lion"; "Lion-Tiger Fight"; "Wild River Safari"; "Hawaii"; "Land of the Pyramids"; "Belles of the South Seas"; "Mexico"; "Bali"; "Paris"; "Caribbean-Holiday"; "Romantic Italy"; and many others. These are obtainable in both 8mm and 16mm.

†A newly developed 16mm camera sound system is the Auricon Cine-Voice. It makes perfectly synchronized sound movies so easy that any hobbyist can produce them without difficulty. The cheap model has a capacity for 200 feet. The larger model, with a capacity for 1200 feet, is strictly for Houston oil magnates.

rapher who travels. Bulk and weight, not to speak of supplies and repairs (the more elaborate the equipment the greater the maintenance problem)—rule it out.

Yet it must be admitted that there have been enthusiasts who have given me the lie in this matter and have carted such equipment along with them on the most extensive trips. "Very much worth while," they say.

MOVIE-MAKING EQUIPMENT TO TAKE WITH YOU

What kind of movie-making equipment to take with him is of the first importance to the tourist. The important features for him to consider are cost, bulk and weight, and, finally, the availability of film supply while traveling. It's a positive fact that 8mm film is more readily available than 16mm because, in foreign countries, with a lower standard of living than ours, the average movie photographer cannot afford the expense of 16mm films; so less of it is stocked. Sometimes it's not available at all. However, nearly every country has at least one important distributor who will be able to supply the larger size. (See list of foreign photo dealers, page 73.)

Another element that will figure in the decision the movie photographer will make is lens speed. If he anticipates taking pictures in poor light he will need the fastest lens available. Lenses for movie cameras come as fast as f/1.5. Many photographers are quite content with f/2.7; it is the lens equipment on the Eastman Brownie Cine Camera.

Of course, f/1.5 will take satisfactory pictures in very poor light indeed, especially when used in conjunction with fast panchromatic film; but color does not show to good advantage in poor light so it would be a tactical error to depend on a fast lens alone to produce good color movies.

Magazine Loading

The tourist photographer will also have to choose between the advantages of magazine loading against the ordinary camera in which you have to thread and load yourself. As the term implies, the magazine-loading camera is a camera for which film, already loaded and threaded into a magazine, is supplied. All the user has to do is to open the camera and slide the magazine into the compartment provided for it; a child could do it. It is simpler, even, than putting roll film into a still box camera. Excellent for indolent or two-thumbed people.

Magazine loading has another advantage. It is an advantage so decisive that it induces photographers, who have no hesitancy about loading their own, to choose magazine loading instead. Since the film is always safe in its own light-tight container, you can change magazines without having to expose all the film in it; thus you can switch from black and white to color and vice versa whenever the change is desired.

But this convenience costs something, both in initial camera cost and in film cost; film in the magazine holder is more expensive than the self-loading kind. Besides, loading your own film is not difficult; damage to the film in the process is not frequent, when due care is exercised.

As with the still camera, 3-D is splashing into the moving picture and many cameras making use of the three-dimension technique are already in existence while new ones are being developed daily by manufacturers anxious to profit by its novelty. Projectors for viewing in 3 dimensions are coming along rapidly too.*

You might be interested in movie cameras which mount several lenses on a revolving turret so that one can quickly shift into place different lenses for varying distance shots and with which it is possible to produce a variety of trick effects with the facility of professional equipment. Some of these cameras, indeed, are truly professional and almost match the most elaborate Hollywood equipment. But luxurious apparatus like this requires a fat checkbook.

You may also have to decide between different kinds of viewing; between cameras which have simple subject viewing and those boasting reflex (ground glass) viewing through the lens. Each has its followers; individual taste is the governing factor in the choice.

Another feature of some movie cameras is the ability to take single-frame pictures. In effect this converts the movie camera into a still camera and might eliminate the necessity to carry a still camera along with you on your trip. However, there is the complication that you will have to cut out the individual frame for making prints and then re-splice the film. Further, since the single frame is a positive, it will be necessary to make a negative from it before you can make a print. Eating your cake and having it too can sometimes produce indigestion, photographically, as well as in any other way.†

Movie-Making Accessories

Movie cameras can have as many accessories as do still cameras. Mostly, these accessories are for the purpose of enabling the user to produce some of Hollywood's trick effects, such as "fade-ins," "dissolves," "montages," and a host of others. On more expensive cameras many of the devices for producing these effects have been built in. It is a moot

---

*It is not necessary to buy an entirely new camera for 3-D; accessory devices are available to convert your present camera to the technique. Among such are the systems offered by Elgeet Co., 834 Smith St., Rochester, N.Y. (attachment for camera and projector). Paillard Products Co., New York City (importers of the famous Bolex camera) offers a similar system.

†The only apparent advantage would be the elimination of the still camera. However, if one were to be satisfied with the tiny 16mm negative thus supplied, there are fairly good still cameras which yield tiny negatives; these cameras are so small they can be carried in a vest pocket. Some have lenses whose resolving power yields negatives that can be enlarged 15 times with good definition. And their cost is small.

MOVIE-MAKING EQUIPMENT TO TAKE WITH YOU 105

question whether it is better to buy a camera in which these are already incorporated or to buy the necessary accessories separately as the need or desire for them develops — and as your oil dividends come in.*

Not to be overlooked, though not inexpensive, are movie cameras employing the Zoomar lens. This employs a technique allowing variable focus (near and far) and provides amazing versatility and convenience.

So you see there are many angles to consider before making your purchase. The very first angle that will affect your decision is film size. You might start with 8mm equipment and, later, develop a preference for 16mm because of its larger image.

If you do, you will practically throw away your investment in 8mm film-making: projector, screen, etc. While the machinery may be traded, what are you going to do with film you've made and collected, some of it undoubtedly of great sentimental value? Of course, it's possible to have the 8mm collection transferred to 16mm film in the laboratory, but that will represent a sizeable item of cost.

This is not to discourage the purchase of 8mm equipment. Many movie-makers have stuck with it and continue to be satisfied. You will finally have to decide between the two sizes on the basis of cost, since 8mm results are by no means inferior to 16mm. Also, in the 8mm size you can get the very inexpensive Brownie movie camera and its related equipment, which boasts not only extreme simplicity but also offers the least expensive movie outfit one can get.

An accessory of great interest is the Pan Cinor variable focal length lens. With a quick turn of the wrist this lens can range all the way from 20mm to 60mm. This eliminates the necessity to change lenses for varying distances; it also allows for trick effects. It can be installed on most of the popular 16mm cameras in use. This accessory is distributed by Paillard Products, 106 6th Avenue, New York City.

GOING THROUGH CUSTOMS
At Home and Abroad

The American tourist accustomed to the free-and-easy life at home may set out on his trip on the assumption that his movements abroad may be as free and easy as at home and that the regulations dealing with photography are as casual as our own. The fact is that neither assumption is true. Every country has its individual customs procedure and crossing borders may be easy or it may be as technical as making love to a Latin-American senorita.

As a matter of fact, while it is true that an American may travel through our entire country without care, it is nevertheless a fact that when he returns to the U.S. from abroad, he has to go through our own quite arduous customs examination. This, while tedious enough for an American citizen, is considered by foreigners who have gone through it an outrageously difficult matter — far more difficult than their own customs procedure, they aver.*

Even when the tourist crosses borders into a country not particularly friendly to our own, the officials have a healthy respect for the dollars the tourist will spend in their country and they will usually be courteous and reasonable enough. If your behaviour is correct, they are likely to interpret their regulations in a liberal manner and may even stretch a point in your behalf, since they have considerable discretion.

Most of the European countries will make only a superficial examination of your belongings anyway and will accept an *oral* declaration. The average tourist has no reason to take advantage of this looseness, so unlike our own, and should be circumspect enough to bring along only what is obviously legal and exempt from duty.

Invariably, foreign countries limit the importation of certain items. Cigarettes (with which we have nothing to do here) are one such item. Photographic supplies are another. If one follows the regulations rigidly, you would be limited to very little photographic activity. Actually, many tourists bring in considerably more than regulations allow, yet I've never heard of any American getting into difficulties on that account.

---

*Off the record, I have rarely spent more than 15 minutes at any foreign customs examination. On the other hand, I've never been through an American customs examination in less than an hour; usually it's been closer to 2 hours. Many have experienced as much as 4 hours delay during busy tourist seasons, so the foreigners have a point.

It is true that most photographic supplies are readily available in foreign countries, the name Kodak being almost a dictionary word throughout the world, but color film (still and movie) is often difficult to obtain in Europe and perhaps impossible in the more backward countries. You can obtain European-made color film but it's not the same as ours (as explained elsewhere) and it furnishes processing complications.

Even if you are able to obtain American-made color film abroad and wish to send it to the U.S. for processing, it is subject to American duty because it was purchased abroad and the duty has to be paid by anyone receiving it in the U.S. in your absence. Also American-*bought* film, if sent to the U.S. in *foreign containers,* will also have duty levied on it. American authorities are not fussy about determining whether it is American film or not, or whether it was bought in the U.S.; the foreign container stamps its identity as far as they are concerned.

In any case, *foreign* color film had best be processed abroad. If you do this it will avoid complications and, besides, it gives you a chance to assess the results you are getting.

An important thing to do with regard to our own Customs Bureau —and one that will avoid great inconvenience to you on your return— is to register all your foreign-made equipment with the Customs Department in the U.S. *before* leaving.* Many of the cameras used in the U.S. have a foreign origin and yours may be one such. The fact that you bought it in the U.S. will not clear it coming back unless you do register it here. If, in the rush of going away, you neglect to do this, at least carry with you the bill of sale showing where you purchased the equipment. The same document may ease things for you abroad too.

Of course, any equipment you buy abroad, while on your trip, is subject to American duty. These duties in turn are subject to your personal exemption as a tourist — up to $500 per person at the present time.

If the total of your purchases abroad does not exceed that amount, you may consider the photographic apparatus bought abroad free of duty. If you are traveling with your wife or children, you may add the total of their exemptions to yours as well.

---

201 Varick St., N.Y., is the place in New York where registration can be made.

CUSTOMS REGULATIONS

of Various Foreign Countries With Respect to Photographic Equipment

Austria   One camera of any type per person duty-free. Film in reasonable quantity for personal use and not for sale permitted. The same amount is permitted to be taken out. Film may be mailed out for processing.

Australia   One still and one movie camera per person, as used personal effects, duty-free. Exposed, undeveloped film is subject to censorship before sending out. There is also difficulty about receiving processed film from outside.
(New Zealand regulations are the same)

Argentina—Reasonable amount of equipment and supplies for personal use and not for resale permitted duty-free.

Belgium   Visitors are allowed to bring in one camera with a maximum of 12 plates or one roll film. Also one movie camera of amateur size and one roll of film for same. Equipment must have the appearance of being used, otherwise liable to duty which amount, however, is returned on leaving the country with the equipment. Exposed film may be taken out or sent out for processing.

Brazil   Reasonable quantity of equipment and supplies for personal use and not for sale.

Chile   Same as above

Colombia   Same as above

Cuba   Same as above.

Denmark   Visitors allowed to bring in one still and one amateur movie camera. Also *ample* (official wording) supply of film for same. No restriction on sending out film for processing or receiving same from outside. Expect liberal interpretation.

Eire   Same as Denmark.

England   While, theoretically, all equipment and film are subject to duty, it is rarely exacted. Examining customs official has full discretion.

Finland   No restrictions of any kind for film and equipment, if declared for personal use, and not for resale.

Egypt   One still and one movie camera allowed duty-free. Only limited amount of film allowed. There may be difficulty in sending film out for processing and same is true about receiving processed film from outside the country. All equipment must be taken out of the country within a year or is subject to duty. All equipment must be declared. Regulations may be subject to change and possibly duty exacted on equipment.

France One still and one movie camera per person. One roll of film for each camera. No restriction on sending film out of the country for processing and no restriction on receiving processed film. Professional photographers are subject to numerous provisions; they would find it expedient to assume amateur status.

Guatemala—Despite the tendentious stories heard about Guatemala there are practically no restrictions on the importation of equipment or supplies. And no restrictions on sending film out for processing and receiving same.

Hawaii Practically no restrictions for Americans. Film and equipment of all kinds are in full supply and easily obtainable.

Israel Unlimited supply of equipment and film may be brought in and out. Supplies in Israel very short so tourists are advised to bring in as much as they may need. No restrictions on sending film out or receiving it back.

Italy Practically no restrictions, in reasonable quantity, and for personal use.

India One still and one movie camera duty-free. Reasonable amount of film. Export license required for sending out for processing. However, interpretations of regulations are liberal. Eastman headquarters can be of much assistance.

Japan No restrictions of any kind.

Mexico No restrictions, if in reasonable quantity. There is little difficulty in sending film out for processing but there is some difficulty about receiving processed film from outside.

Netherlands Practically no restrictions — in reasonable quantity and for personal use.

Norway "Photographic equipment with accessories for taking moving pictures as well as raw film, etc., may be imported by American visitors duty free against written declaration to the effect that such articles are for personal use while in the country and will be taken out on departure." No restrictions on sending film out for processing.

Panama No restrictions if in reasonable amount for personal use and not for sale.

Portugal "Visitors can bring in, free of duty, a small amount of film as well as one still and one movie camera of amateur format. This does not hold for photographic equipment for professional use." No restrictions on sending film out for processing but receipt of any film from outside subject to duty. Any equipment in excess of the amount allowed duty free is subject to duty but the amount of duty is returned on leaving the counry with the equipment on which duty has been levied, if within a reasonable period of time.

Philippines Practically no restrictions.

Peru Practically no restrictions if in reasonable quantity.

Porto Rico No restrictions of any kind.

Spain Practically no restrictions if in reasonable quantity.

Sweden One still and one amateur movie camera duty free. Film subject to duty. Export license required for sending film out for processing but duty may be charged when the processed film comes back. All of the equipment brought into the country must be taken out on departure. Reasonable amount of film can be brought in when entering the country.

Switzerland One still and one movie camera of amateur size permitted duty free per person. Two rolls of film may be brought in for personal use and not for sale. No restrictions on sending film out for processing but duty may be charged when it comes back. All equipment brought into the country must be taken out on departure. Many tourists have brought in more film than is legally specified, without difficulty.

South Africa One still and one movie camera duty free; also reasonable amount of film. Some difficulty in sending film out for processing and receiving same. All equipment must be taken out within one year or subject to duty. Film scarce so bring in plenty.

All the regulations quoted above must be interpreted in the light of a memorandum I received from the official tourist information office of a prominent European country.

"We are sorry if the rules on the import of cameras and film seem severe but we know from experience that the customs official in charge, to whom is left a great deal of judgment, is very lenient in this respect, especially when Americans are concerned. We seriously doubt that anyone will have any difficulty importing photographic material for personal use even if it is in excess of the amount allowed by the regulations, unless the quantity seems large enough to suggest trade purposes."

I have nothing to add to the foregoing except to say that it bears out my own experience and the experience of many travelers whom I know.

If you should get into any difficulty — if, for example, it is ruled that you have more apparatus or material than is allowed in a given country duty-free — you have two alternatives.

(1) You can leave the excess material at the Customs House of entry to be reclaimed on departure from the country. If you plan to leave the country at another point than the place where your material is to

be stored, you can have the material forwarded, under bond, by a reputable forwarding agency to the point of departure. This can be done before you actually leave the country; in that case, the material will be stored at the customs house at the point of departure instead of at the point of entry.

(2) You could register the material and have it forwarded to the customs house at the next country on your itinerary to await your arrival there.

In either case, you will incur not only the cost of transportation from point to point (which is nominal) but you will also be liable for storage charges wherever the material is held. These charges are also nominal but over a prolonged period, they can mount up annoyingly.

There is another point about which a cautionary suggestion is advisable. It is the usual procedure, when going through foreign customs, for porters to grab your luggage and take it to the proper departments for the customs examination. To inexperienced tourists, this procedure is not only confusing but alarming.

But do not worry; when the ordeal is over, you will find your luggage all right, even though it may have seemed to disappear; the porter will find you — that's his business. As I advised in another book,* the apparently confusing procedure is a very useful service indeed because a good porter can expedite matters for you amazingly.

However — and here's the caution — do not surrender to the porter your *photographic equipment;* carry it to the customs shed yourself. By doing this, you will avoid damage and possible loss. When you notice the rough manner with which baggage is handled, even by the best-intentioned porter, you'll realize the wisdom of this suggestion.

Speak-Easy, Dine-Easy, Tip-Easy, Save-Easy (Harian Pub., Greenlawn, N.Y.)

HOW TO INSURE YOUR PHOTOGRAPHIC EQUIPMENT AGAINST LOSS OR DAMAGE

If you are a prudent traveler, you will insure your baggage against loss and its contents against damage. While the hazards are not great, there always exists the possibility that you will incur losses and it is wise to provide for that contingency.

Baggage insurance covers all losses sustained for personal belongings whether inside the baggage at the time the loss was sutained or not. Seemingly, that would cover your photographic equipment. But a little calculation will prove that it would be more expedient to carry separate insurance on photographic equipment.

The present rate for baggage insurance (and personal belongings as part of the baggage) is $2.80 per $100 worth per month. You make your own appraisal of the value of the belongings you wish to insure and the amount of the premium is based on your appraisal.

Since, in many cases, a camera and related equipment might be worth $500 or more, the premium on that part of your belongings, if you want to be fully covered, would come to more than all the rest of your belongings, when based on the baggage insurance rates.

It would be simpler and more economical to take out a separate policy on your photographic equipment under what is known as a "floater" policy and which covers such equipment not only against loss but damage sustained in your own hands. Many a camera has been knocked off the rail of a ship in the process of taking a picture while crossing the ocean. The skipper might stop for a cry of "man overboard" but even a Scotch skipper would not dream of doing so for anything less. Likewise, cameras frequently fall off the racks of speeding trains and are severely damaged.

Insurance rates on a "floater" policy to cover risks of all kinds are not particularly high when measured against the replacement value of the equipment and it's no fun taking your own losses if unfortunate things do happen.

Therefore, it's a good policy to have a good policy.

Not all insurance companies handle this business; it's fairly new to the insurance field. Your broker can take care of the matter for you. However, if you do not have a broker, insurance companies will issue a policy to you directly, though there is no saving in eliminating the broker.

How To Insure Your Photographic Equipment

The Hartford Fire Insurance Co., Hartford, Conn., is a leading company handling such business. And insurance companies handling such business are scattered throughout Europe, in Switzerland, especially. In England, a reliable company is the Norwich Union (Camera Insurance Dept.) P.O. Box 4, Norwich, Norfolk, England.

I might mention that baggage insurance in general can be obtained from Swiss companies at lower rates than from American companies and the matter can be arranged by mail. Experience with Swiss companies has been very satisfactory. A reliable Swiss company is: *Die Schweitz, Allgemeine Versicherungsgesellschaft*. Their American agent is Ernst Hoffman, 55 Liberty Street, New York City.

A "floater" policy covering your equipment against all losses, under all circumstances (except as noted in fine print in the body of the policy) will cost, on the average about 5¢ per day for each $1000 worth of protection. Such policies are issued for a year but protection for longer periods can be arranged, doubtlessly.

It doesn't require much calculation to determine how much cheaper this rate is than the rate required to cover the equipment in the policy covering baggage and personal belongings.

If it is desired to insure for only a short period, the most practical method is to take out the policy for a year (as normally issued) and cancel in writing to the company at the time the travel period is over. Then you are charged the *earned* premium and the unused balance of the premium is returned to you. Naturally, the premium for a period shorter than a year is relatively higher. Because of that fact, it's likely you'll decide to have the policy run for the full year.

Since any policy only offers to recover replacement value of equipment covered, it is obvious that there is no recovery for damage due to usage, that is, for normal wear and tear. There is also an escape clause (in the fine print) excepting loss from damage resulting from riots, insurrection, or action by any governmental authority such as seizure or confiscation under quarantine or customs regulations or during a state of war.

Policies are also judged invalid if they have been issued on the basis of any misrepresentation by the assured, or attempted fraud either before or after a loss.

Claims must be made within 90 days of loss or damage, and failure to do so may invalidate the claim. Claims are usually paid within 60 days of valid claims, a valid claim being defined as presentation of satisfactory proof of the loss. Amount of payment is based on the value of the equipment at the time the loss or damage was sustained.

The interpretation of all these technical provisions in small type may be liberal or rigid, depending on the company and circumstances. Experience indicates that the assured need not worry too much about these subordinate details. Insurance companies do not generally take advantage of them unnecessarily.

Outside house of Ravel at Montport L'Amaury

SECTION OF GENERAL TECHNICAL DATA

Table of Lens Openings and Exposure Factors

Lens opening	f/1.5	f/2	f/2.8	f/3.5	f/4.5	f/5.6	f/8	f/11	f/16	f/22	f/32
Exposure	1000	500	250	125	80	60	25	10	5	2	1*

It will be noted that, except for f/4.5 (which is really an in-between stop) all exposures double with each change of stop.

The f/ numbers represent lens diaphragm stops or openings and all cameras except box cameras have the lenses marked off in these f/ numbers. The f/ numbers listed here are the ones to be found on all American cameras, and foreign cameras which are exported to the U.S.

On the Continent, you can find cameras with different lens stops (openings) though they are not common. While this may be of only academic interest to Americans it is well known that the European lens stops also double their exposures from stop to stop. Therefore the table above is a fair guide for gauging the exposures on Continental cameras too.

For example: when you shift from f/1.5 (the first stop listed), with its exposure of 1/1000th of a second, to the next smaller stop, f/2, you must increase exposure to 1/500th of a second. And as you keep on from stop to stop, you must increase the exposure according to the lower line of figures. Remember, as lens opening *numbers* increase, the opening *decreases;* as exposure numbers (lower line) *decrease,* exposure time *increases.*

---

*All numbers except this one are fractions of a second; the 1 represents a full second.

BASIC DAYLIGHT EXPOSURES*
—for most commonly used films

	Bright sun	Cloudy sun	Shade	Deep shade or interior near window
Triple S Pan (sheet Film) or film rated 200 (D)**	f32 1/50 f22 1/100 f16 1/250 f11 1/500 f8 1/1000	f32 1/10 f22 1/25 f16 1/50 f11 1/75 f8 1/250 f5.6 1/500 f3.5 1/1000	f32 1/2 f22 1/5 f16 1/10 f11 1/25 f8 1/250 f5.6 1/100 f3.5 1/200 f2.8 1/500 f2 1/1000	f32 1/10 f22 1/25 f16 1/50 f11 1/100 f8 1/250 f5.6 1/500 f3.5 1/1000
Tri-X or film rated 200 (D)	f32 1/50 f22 1/100 f16 1/250 f11 1/500 f8 1/1000	f32 1/10 f22 1/25 f16 1/50 f11 1/75 f8 1/250 f5.6 1/500 f3.5 1/1000	f32 1/2 f22 1/5 f16 1/10 f11 1/25 f8 1/250 f5.6 1/100 f3.5 1/200 f2.8 1/500 f2 1/1000	f32 1/10 f22 1/25 f16 1/50 f11 1/100 f8 1/250 f5.6 1/500 f3.5 1/1000
Plus X or film rated 80 (D)**	f32 1/25 f22 1/50 f16 1/75 f11 1/150 f8 1/250	f32 1/4 f22 1/10 f16 1/50 f11 1/60 f8 1/150 f5.6 1/250 f3.5 1/400	f32 1 sec. f22 1/2 sec. f16 1/4 f11 1/10 f8 1/15 f5.6 1/40 f3.5 1/75 f2.8 1/150 f2 1/300	f16 1/2 sec. f11 1/4 f8 1/10 f5.6 1/20 f3.5 1/50 f2.8 1/75 f2 1/150
Color Film rated 32 (D)	f22 1/2 f16 1/25 f11 1/60 f8 1/100 f5.6 1/200 f3.5 1/500	f16 1/4 f11 1/10 f8 1/25 f5.6 1/60 f3.5 1/150 f2.8 1/250	f8 1/4 f5.6 1/10 f3.5 1/25 f2.8 1/60 f2 1/150	f5.6 1/2 f3.5 1/10 f2.8 1/20 f2 1/25
Movie Film *** rated 100 (D)	f22 or f16 depending on subject	f16 or f11 depending on subject	f6.3	f3.5
Movie Pan Film *** rated 50 (D)	f11 or f8 depending on subject	f8 or f5.6 depending on subject	f5.6 or f4.5 depending on subject	f2.5 or f2 depending on subject
Movie Color Film *** rated 10 (D)	f8 or f5.6 depending on subject	f4 or 3.5 depending on subject	f2.8	

*Time exposures cannot be calculated, the individual subject and its lighting conditions being primary factors. This table may give a rough basis, after which the experiment becomes empirical. Luckily, black and white film has such latitude that mild errors will still produce useable negatives.

**See film speed ratings on page 121. Black and white film purchased abroad will contain inside the package the film speed rating and, generally, its conversion to American film speeds.

***Based on 16 frames per second. For 8 frames, close down one stop; for 32 frames, open up one stop.

TECHNICAL DATA 119

Guide to f/ numbers

to be used in conjunction with Flash Guide Numbers

Here is a cute formula supplied by General Electric's Lamp Division. It is simple to remember and, once it is mastered, you are quickly in control of every situation where flash lighting is used.

A short cut to correct exposure with flash is built into every camera that has an adjustable diaphragm. The first step is simply to set the camera diaphragm (lens number) to the proper f/ number for an 11 foot shot, according to the *guide number* for the film, the shutter speed, and the bulb that are being used.

For example: With an exposure guide number of 175; at 11 feet, that would be f/16 $(\frac{175}{11})$. The guide number 175 dvides by the distance 11; result, f/16.

Now notice how the f/number changes as you move either way from an 11-foot shooting distance:

F/number	f/32	f/22	f/16	f/11	f/8	f/5.6	f/4
Distance	5.6 ft.	8 ft.	11 ft.	16 ft.	22 ft.	32 ft.	45 ft.

When you move your flash *closer* a distance in feet equal to one f/stop (from 11 ft. to 8 ft.), *close down* one f/stop. If you *increase* your distance an amount equal to one f/stop (from 11 ft. to 16 ft.), *open up* one f/stop.

No matter where you start, on a stop or between stops, according to the guide number, set the camera diaphragm first at the proper position for an 11 foot shot. You now get correct exposure if you move the setting up or down the space of one stop each time your distance changes by an amount equalling one f/stop.

Of course, you must use shooting distances equal to f/stops: 5-5.6 ft. – 7-*8* ft. – 10-*11* ft. – 15-*16* ft. – 20-*22* ft. – 30-*32* ft. Should you forget, the f/number scale on your camera is always there to remind you.

EXPOSURE TABLE FOR PHOTOFLOOD LAMPS**

This is a Guide Number table to be used for black and white films. To find the f number (lens opening or diaphragm) locate the proper *guide number* for your film's ASA speed rating, shutter speed and lamp. Then divide that *guide number* by distance in feet from the lamp to subject. The answer is the f/ number to use.

ASA Tungsten Film Speed Ratings		Guide Numbers							
		8	10	12	16	20	25 to 32	50 to 64	100	200 to 250
Lamp	Shutter Speed									
One #1 Flood	1 sec.	53	60	64	75	85	110	150	200	300
	1/5	24	26	29	34	38	48	65	90	130
	1/25	11	12	13	15	17	21	30	40	60
	Movie*	10	11	12	14	16	19	25	38	50
	1/50	8	8	9	11	12	15	20	30	40
	1/100	6	6	7	8	8	11	15	20	30
Two #1 or One #2	1 sec.	75	85	90	100	120	150	210	290	420
	1/5	33	38	40	48	50	68	100	130	180
	1/25	15	17	18	21	23	30	40	60	80
	Movie*	14	15	17	19	22	27	35	55	75
	1/50	11	12	13	15	17	21	30	40	60
	1/100	7	8	9	11	12	15	20	30	40
Two #2	1 sec.	105	120	130	150	165	210	300	415	590
	1/5	48	52	58	68	75	95	135	185	250
	1/25	21	23	26	30	35	42	60	85	120
	Movie*	20	21	24	27	30	38	55	75	110
	1/50	15	17	19	21	23	30	40	60	80
	1/100	10	12	13	15	16	20	30	40	60

*Based on average speed: 16 frames per second. Based on the use of black and white movie film.

**Note that this table is for guide numbers only. Tables for actual exposures and lamp placing are given on page . The average photographer may find those tables quicker and simpler to follow, though the table above is basic, and well worth mastering.

MOST POPULAR FILM SPEEDS

(ASA ratings)

These film speed ratings will help find the proper exposure guide for the film you are using when employing flash bulbs or photo flood lamps. The Tungsten (T) speed is the one to use for artificial lighting. (D) is the rating for daylight use.

35MM AND MINIATURE CAMERA FILM	D	T
ANSCO		
Ultra Speed Pan	100	64
Supreme	50	32
GEVAERT		
Panchromosa	80	50
Microgran	24	16

ROLL FILMS AND FILM PACKS	D	T
ANSCO		
Superpan Press	125	80
Supreme	50	32
Plenachrome	50	25
ILFORD		
HPS*	400	160
HP3	250	200
FP3	100	64
KODAK		
Tri-X	250	80
Panatomic X	25	20
Verichrome Pan	80	64
GEVAERT		
Superchrome	50	25

SHEET FILMS	D	T
ANSCO		
Triple S Pan	200	160
Superpan Press	125	80
Isopan	50	32
Superpan Portrait	50	32
Triple S Ortho	125	64

DUPONT	D	T
High Speed Pan-type 428	160	125
Arrow Pan	160	125
XF Pan	64	40
XF Ortho	64	32
KODAK	D	T
Tri X Pan	200	160
Super XX	100	80
Panatomic X	32	25
Ortho X	125	64
Super Panchro Press Type B	125	100
Portrait Pan	64	40
Super Ortho Press	100	50
GEVAERT		
Panchromosa	80	50
Pan Portrait	64	40
Superchrome	50	25
ILFORD	D	T
HP3	250	200
KODAK	D	T
Super XX	100	80
Plus X	50	40
DUPONT		
Superior 2	50	40
Superior 3	100	30

—continued on next page

*This latest Ilford product is sensational. I have personally verified its unbelievable speed, using its processing recommendations and my own formula. In both instances, graininess was really minimized in this high-speed emulsion.

Most popular film speeds—continued

COLOR FILM	D	T	MOVIE FILM	D	T
ANSCOCHROME			**ANSCO**		
Sheet Film			16 mm—		
Daylight Type	32	12*	Hypan	40	32
Tungsten Type	..	12	Supreme	50	32
35 mm			8 mm—		
Daylight Type	32	12*	Twin 8		
Tungsten Type	..	12	Hypan	40	32
16 mm			**DUPONT**		
Daylight	10	..	16 mm—Negative		
Tungsten	..	10	Type 901	40	32
Roll Film			Negative		
Daylight	10	..	Type 914	40	25
Tungsten Type	..	12			
			GEVAERT		
KODAK			Ultra Pan	80	64
Ektachrome ..			Super Pan	25	16
Sheet and Roll Film					
Daylight (Process			**KODAK**		
E-2)	32	12*	16 mm—Cine-Kodak		
Type B	5	8	Super XX	100	80
Kodachrome Film			Cine-Kodak		
Daylight Type	10	5	Super X	40	32
Type F	..	12	8 mm—		
Kodacolor Roll Film			Kodak		
Daylight Type	32	25	Super X	40	32
Type A	..	20			

Sensational Advance in Color Film

Since this book was written, American film manufacturers have not only matched the sensational speed of the British Ilford black and white rollfilm for amateur use, but have surpassed it. Thus, Super XX has been discontinued and Tri-X (Daylight 200, Tungsten 80) substituted.

Even more sensational has been the advance in color film. Popular sizes in color roll film can now be had at the unprecedented speed of 32 ASA against the old speed of 10-12 ASA. Tungsten rating would be about half the daylight rating.

Of course, the new speed does not enable a photographer to picture a dark-colored cat, at midnight, in a coal cellar, but it does make the use of color film more flexible and enlarges photographic possibilities considerably. For example: shutter speeds can be doubled or tripled or (what comes to the same thing) one can close down camera lens one or more stops.

This makes an f/3.5 lens the equivalent of f/2.8 or f/2. Or an f/4.5 lens the equivalent of an f/3.5.

It must be noted, too, that all Eastman color film can now be processed at any commercial laboratory, since revised film prices do not include processing by Eastman laboratories. Eastman laboratory processing is still available at extra cost; the cost would be about the same as the prices prevailing at outside laboratories.

The advantage for Americans in the new arrangement is that travelers abroad will not need to send their color film back to U.S. for processing but can avail themselves of the processing services of suitably equipped laboratories in foreign countries, listed on pages 73-74-75.

TECHNICAL DATA

INSTRUCTIONS FOR PROCESSING COLOR FILM

Roll and 35mm Film

Agitate, the film thoroughly when first placed in solution and agitate for 15 seconds during each minute of the remaining time.

In Total Darkness or Indirect Green Safelight

1. FIRST DEVELOPER. Develop Daylight or Tungsten Type Color Film 19 minutes at 68F (20C). After processing six 20-exposure 35mm or 120 rolls per quart of solution, increase developing time to 20 minutes.

2. SHORTSTOP. 1 minute at 68F (20C). Agitate continuously for 30 seconds.

3. HARDENER. 4 minutes at 68F (20C). Agitate continuously for first minute.

Room Lights May be Turned on and Left on for Remainder of Processing

4. WASH. 3 minutes in running water at 60-75F (16-24C).

5. SECOND EXPOSURE. Expose film to light from a No. 2 floodlamp at a distance of 3 feet for 3 minutes, 1½ minutes on each side.

6. COLOR DEVELOPER. Develop Daylight and Tungsten Type Ansco Color Film 16 minutes in Color Developer at 68F (20C).

7. SHORTSTOP. 1 minute at 68F (20C). (Use same solution as after First Developer.) Agitate continuously for first 30 seconds.

8. HARDENER. 4 minutes at 68F (20C). (Use same solution as after First Developer.) Agitate continuously for first minute.

9. WASH. 5 minutes in running water at 60-75F (16-24C).

10. BLEACH. 5 minutes at 68F (20C). After processing four 8x 10" films or six 120 rolls per quart of solution, increase bleach time to 8 minutes.

11. WASH. 3 minutes in running water at 60-75F (16-24C).

12. FIXER. 4 minutes at 68F (20C) with agitation.

13. WASH. 10 minutes in running water at 60-75F (16-24C). If the water is below 60F, the washing time should be increased to 15 minutes.

14. DRYING. Wipe gently with clean damp chamois or viscose sponge and hang to dry in a cool, dust-free place. For more even and rapid drying, dip film into a 0.1% detergent solution (such as Glim) for 10 seconds. The film may then be hung up to dry without wiping with a chamois or sponge.

	Processing Capacity		
Size of Outfit	20 Ex. 35mm	828 Roll	120 Roll
1 Quart	8	20	8
1 Gallon	32	80	32
3½ Gallon	112	280	112

Ansco Color Processing Equipment

Ansco Color Film may be processed in trays or tanks made of materials commonly used for photographic purposes, such as glass, rubber, ceramic or Type 316 stainless steel.

Daylight tanks can be used in the ordinary manner, that is, pouring in the various solutions and emptying the tank after the specified time has elapsed. After the second exposure, the top of the tank need not be replaced since the remaining operations can be carried out in ordinary room light. The self-threading reel with the Ansco Developing Tank was designed so that one flange is transparent, permitting the second exposure to be made without removing the film from the reel. The second exposure is made through the clear flange, exposing for 6 minutes—twice the normal time—shifting the reel around constantly during the exposure to be sure all areas of the film receive sufficient light.

With most other type of reels, the film must be removed from the reel for the second exposure. It can be reloaded onto the reel by submerging both the reel and the film into cold water, using the same technique as though film were dry. This procedure overcomes the difficulty of loading wet film onto plastic type reels.

Partially Processing Ansco Color Film

If it is necessary to store exposed Ansco Color Films for a considerable period of time or under unfavorable conditions of heat and humidity before they can be completely processed or returned to the Ansco Color Laboratory for processing, users should partially process the film. Follow the instructions for First Development and Shortstop, and eliminating the Hardening bath, wash in cool running water (60-75F) for 10 minutes. The film can then be dried in the normal way. Resume processing with "Second Exposure"—step 5.

If the films are returned to Binghamton for completion of the processing, the package must be clearly marked "Films partially processed—development should start with color developing." Films not so marked will be given complete processing and irretrievably spoiled.

Occasionally, blemishes will occur in color film, not only during the course of processing, but years afterwards, with aging. The following firms can remove such blemishes and can coat the film with a preparation that guards against future blemishes and acts as a preservative as well:

Bailey Films Co., Los Angeles, Cal.
Swank Motion Picture Co., St. Louis, Mo.
Delta Visual Service, New Orleans, La.
International Film Bureau, Chicago, Ill.

Eastman Co. is not behind the Ansco in amateur processing developments. Thus, Kodak color film, vastly improved technically, makes possible amateur processing in color. Eastman still is available for the processing but advanced amateurs can now "roll their own".

TONING PRINTS

This is an interesting effect that can lift a black and white subject out of the ordinary class. Toned prints can be made in a large variety of colors and shades other than black. And it can be done at your convenience — it need not be done at the same time as the original print is made. What you can do is to collect a number of prints that pictorial analysis indicates would be enhanced by the process and do them all at one time.

A large number of prepared chemicals are sold for the purpose or you can prepare your own formula if you wish to experiment — but why bother? The prepared chemicals are so much more convenient. The two most popular toners used are sulfide and selenium.

Toners have different effects on different papers and, in addition, their effectiveness will be governed to a considerable extent by the development and fixing of the original print. You will have some difficulty with prints that have been fixed with a hardening bath in the original processing. Such prints may well defy your attempts at satisfactory toning.

Therefore, if you have any thought about toning a particular print later on, do not use a hardening ingredient in fixing that print. When, after some experimenting, you have hit on a toning solution and a photographic paper that yield the effects that please you, stick to that combination for all your toning work.

If you are an experienced amateur, you may ignore this advice because, most likely, you will have come to the conclusion (and rightfully) that some tones suit some subjects better than others; while other subjects look better with still other tones. Indeed, this technique is one of the most interesting in photography and its effects are susceptible to unlimited variety. So, if you want to experiment, here's your chance.

Rural scene in Switzerland

OTHER HARIAN BOOKS

AMERICA BY CAR—planned routings to the best in the U.S., Canada, and Mexico.

The book that takes you to all the 4-star sights in whatever corner of the U.S., Canada, or Mexico you drive to. Road by road, it tells the scenic way to go, and it always directs you to the important sights along the way and in the cities. Plus thousands of recommendations for where to eat and stay. $2.50.

BARGAIN PARADISES OF THE WORLD

This is a book on how to double what your money can buy. For that is what spending a few weeks or months, or even retiring, in the world's bargain paradises amouns to: places like the West Indies, Mexico, South America, the healthful islands of the South Seas, the marvelous Balearic Islands where two can live like kings for less han $50 a week. For a life of luxuries on what you'd get only necessities back home, send for this book. $1.50.

OFF-THE-BEATEN PATH

This book names the really low-cost Florida retirement and vacationing towns, the best values in Texas, the Southwest, California, the South and East, Canada — and a dozen other areas which the crowds have not yet discovered. You read of island paradises, art colonies (artists search for picturesque, low-cost locations!), areas with almost a perfect climate. Here are unspoiled seashore villages, tropic-like islands, and dozens of other spots at some of the lowest prices you've heard of since the gone-forever prewar days. 100,000 words and plenty of pictures. Only $2.

MEXICO—WHERE EVERYTHING COSTS LESS

The authentic guide to vacationing for a while or retiring in the most colorful sections of all Mexico, that fabulous land where the dollar buys so much more. Plus full details on how to invest in this country, where banks, real estate, etc., pay better than in the U.S. $1.50.

TODAY'S BEST BUYS IN AMERICAN VACATIONS

Norman Ford's personal selection of the very best vacation buys all over America: dude ranches for less than ordinary resorts, the best buys in moderate cost Florida vacations, old southern inns, low cost modern inns, low cost sports fishing lodges, where to find real French life in Canada, etc. Why take the same stale vacation over and over again? For a new view of America, get this book. $1.50.

WHERE TO RETIRE ON A SMALL INCOME

This book selects only those U.S. communities where living costs are less, the surroundings are pleasant, and nature and the community get together to guarantee a good time from fishing, boating, gardening, concerts, etc. It covers cities, towns, and farms from New England south to Florida, west to California and north to the Pacific Northwest. Some people spend hundreds of dollars trying to get information like this by traveling around. Frequently they fail—there is just too much of America to explore. This book saves you from that danger. Yet it costs only $1.

HOW TO RETIRE ON REAL ESTATE PROFITS

The book that details the kinds of property that pay you best. Answers these and hundreds of other questions: What's the one real estate purchase that stands out above all others to make your income much, much bigger? What is the one best way to let real estate pay your way and live rent free in Florida or California? Do you know how to virtually guarantee your success with a motel (or a less-work trailer park)? In all American history there's never been a better place to put your money than into real estate. So get this book now. $2.

TODAY'S BEST BUYS IN TRAVEL

The best of the thousands of travel tips told to us by our always traveling customers. All are on-the-spot discoveries—a better hotel at less money, a restaurant where good meals cost little, unusual sights not always mentioned in guide books, etc. They will help to cut your travel costs and they will make for a much better trip. $1.50

HOW TO ORDER: See your bookdealer, or if he cannot supply these titles, order direct, enclosing remittance.
Harian Publications, Dept. D, Greenlawn, N. Y.

OTHER HARIAN BOOKS

TRAVEL ROUTES AROUND THE WORLD—the traveler's directory of passenger-carrying freighters

The authentic guide to 700 passenger-carrying freighters to Europe, the West Indies, California, South America, the Far East, around the world. Names the lines, briefly describes the ships, tells where they go, what they cost, etc. $1.

TODAYS BEST BUYS IN FREIGHTER TRAVEL

Norman Ford's own selection of the world's outstanding passenger-carrying freighters. He looked for the comfort of the ship, the good service you'd get, the quality of the meals, the interesting itinerary, the low cost, etc. Freighter travel is the best way to go, and this book helps you pick the world's best freighters. $2.

FREIGHTER DAYS—how to travel by freighter

What your life will be like aboard your passenger-carrying freighter. Don't even think of sailing without this guide to all that's going on around you, how to spend your days aboard your ship, and what to do before you board your freighter. $1.

HOW TO TRAVEL WITHOUT BEING RICH

If you know the seldom-advertised ways of reaching foreign countries, you don't need fantastic sums of money in order to travel. This guide shows you the lower cost, comfortable ways to practically any part of the world. Page after page reveals the ship, rail, bus, airplane, and other routings that save you money and open the world to you. $1.50.

HOW TO GET A JOB THAT TAKES YOU TRAVELING

There's a job waiting for you somewhere—on a ship, with an airline, in foreign or American firms overseas. Here's the full story of the jobs open to you—from jobs in travel agencies to the many opportunities abroad if you will teach English to foreigners. $1.50.

EUROPE ON A SHOESTRING

How to see Europe for considerably less than you think it will cost. All the tricks of touring Europe which you'd normally expect only the man who's been there a dozen times before to know about. Also tells you what to see, how to find the lowest cost tours, etc. $2.

MEXICO AND GUATEMALA BY CAR—the authentic guide to touring these countries where the dollar buys so much more

How to see everything in these colorful countries. With this book you'll never overspend, travel blind, or waste your time on unimportant sights. Plus detailed information on where to get real value in hotels and restaurants, etc. $1.50.

WHERE WILL YOU GO
in Florida or Arizona,
in California or the Southwest,
in Alaska or Hawaii?

None of these states need be expensive—if you know just where to go for whatever you seek. And the guides named below can give you the facts you want. They tell you first of all, road by road, mile by mile, everything you'll find here whether you're on vacation or looking over job, business, real estate, or retirement prospects.

Always, they name the hotels, motels, and restaurants where you can stop for the best accommodations and meals at the price you want to pay. For that longer vacation, they'll show you a real "paradise"—just the spot which has everything you want.

There's much more to these books. If you want a job or a home, they tell you where to head. If you want to retire on a small income, they tell you exactly where you can retire now on the money you've got. Because they always tell you where life is pleasantest on a small income, they can help you take life easy now.

Yet these big books, each with plenty of maps and over 100,000 words, sell for only $2 each—only a fraction of the money you'd spend needlessly if you went here blind. These are the books to help you now:

→ **NORMAN FORD'S FLORIDA.** An enormous guide to this popular state where life can be most delightful. $2.

→ **ALL ABOUT ARIZONA** — the healthful state, where it's great to live and work. $2.

→ **CALIFORNIA — THE STATE THAT HAS EVERYTHING.** $2.

→ **THE HEART OF THE SOUTHWEST.** Where to find absolutely the best in Texas, Colorado, Arizona, and their neighbors. $2.

→ **PACIFIC, U.S.A.** Where to find the best in Alaska, Hawaii, California, and the Pacific Northwest. $2.

HOW TO ORDER: See your bookdealer, or if he cannot supply these titles, order direct, enclosing remittance.
Harian Publications, Dept. D, Greenlawn, N. Y.